Step-by-Step
Patchwork

Step-by-Step Patchwork

Complete instructions for dozens of
patchwork technques including seamed,
mosaic, strip and string, log cabin, crazy
quilt, seminole and appliqué

Helen Fairfield

St. Martin's Press
New York

ISBN 0–312–05278–2

First published in Great Britain as PATCHWORK. 1990

Library of Congress Number: 90–42204

Typeset by Tradespools Ltd, Frome, Somerset

CONTENTS

ACKNOWLEDGEMENT

I should like to thank Beck's Busy Bodies of Byfield, Northamptonshire, for their patience and forbearance whilst being the 'guinea pigs' on which much of this book was tried out; my sister, Joy Purser of Kenosee Lake, Saskatchewan, for ensuring that what I wrote made sense in North America, and the many, many others who were generous with their advice and expertise – particularly Susan Chastney of Northampton, Gisela Thwaites of Newport Pagnell, Wendy Bates of Daventry, Sheila Wilkinson of Amersham, Pauline Rumbold of Weedon, Northamptonshire, and Brenda Power of Hook Norton, Oxfordshire, who lent their work to be photographed.

Peter Haines has again earned my gratitude by producing excellent photographs with the help of Ann Roberts, but my chief thanks for assistance in producing this book must go to my infallible grammarian, proof reader and critic – my husband, Del Fairfield.

Spider Web Variation by Susan Chastney

INTRODUCTION

Patchwork is the joining together of several pieces of material to make a decorative whole. The pieces may be scraps joined together, mosaic-fashion, to make a pattern, or may be applied to a background.

It has been suggested that the first patchwork was made when a worn place on a garment was covered with a patch. It could equally have originated with the joining together of small remnants to make a colourful, patterned covering. Whichever way it happened, economy must have played an important part in patchwork's origins and the tradition of economy has persisted throughout its history.

No one knows when the first patchwork was made, since only a few samples have survived from antiquity. There is, in a Cairo Museum, an Egyptian patchwork canopy of dyed gazelle hide, made some 2,000 years ago. The figure of

1. Pottery figure of a Snake Goddess from Knossos in the Metropolitan Museum of Art, New York

2. Thirteenth-century Spanish illustration to 'Cantigas' by Alphonso the Wise from the Library of the Escorial

the Snake Goddess from Crete, wearing what appears to be a patchwork skirt, is a thousand years older.

Manuscripts and paintings from the Middle Ages onwards show patchwork used for the ceremonial dress of knights and courtiers.

The documented history of modern patchwork really starts at the beginning of the eighteenth century with two surviving specimens, dated within a few years of each other: the Saltonstall quilt in the USA and the Levens Hall quilt and hangings in the North of England. It is obvious that by the time these were made, patchwork was a well practised craft, but no earlier examples have come to light.

In Britain, patchwork tended to remain a cottage craft, seldom found and little appreciated in wealthier homes, except when some quirk of fashion gave it brief popularity.

By contrast, in North America, however humble its beginnings may have been, patchwork has always been appreciated as a useful and decorative craft, valued as much for the thought and effort which went into the making of the quilts as for their utilitarian worth. Even during the 1930s, when handmade items tended to be despised in the new machine age, and in the 1940s, when war work occupied many women who might otherwise have carried on making quilts, the tradition never died out entirely. In fact, some quilts now much sought after in Britain, were shipped over during the war, having been made by members of the Canadian Red Cross for relief of bombed-out Britons.

In the past few decades there has been a revulsion against mass-produced items, and the desire to create something original has re-emerged. The revival of patchwork is a natural result. The simplest forms of patchwork are easy for a beginner to master, and even a first attempt can provide a most satisfying feeling that a new and original artefact has been created.

I can claim to have been involved with patchwork for most of my life. As a small child I remember crouching under the quilting frame in the living-room at home on the Saskatchewan farm where I grew up, retrieving lost needles for my mother and other ladies of the Quilting Bee. When I left home to go to art school I took with me a Grandmother's Fan quilt my mother had made me from the dresses I had worn as a child, and she made similar quilts for each of my sisters, stuffed with the laboriously washed and carded wool from our own sheep.

I must admit that it was many years before I felt the urge to make a quilt myself, but once I had started the addiction took firm hold, and I have been patchworking, quilting and making quilts ever since.

3. *Detail from 'Grandmother's Fan' quilt*

MATERIALS *and* EQUIPMENT

Traditionally, patchwork was made from left-over materials and re-usable scraps. Whilst it is certainly still sensible to make use of left-overs from dressmaking and remnants, as well as the good parts of used garments from jumble sales, it is very important that the fabrics selected should possess certain qualities. They should be:

- Colour fast
- Shrink proof
- Sufficiently opaque for turnings not to show through as shadows on the completed article
- Capable of holding a crease when folded

The fabric which answers best to this description is dress-weight cotton, and it is best to stick to this unless it is quite impossible to find the colours and prints you want in it. Whilst it is possible to use polyester/cotton, it lacks the last two qualities.

Any fabric to be used for patchwork should be washed before use to ensure that it is colour fast and that it will not shrink after it has been made up. Light fastness is always a problem, as manufacturers do not seem to consider that dress materials need to be fade proof. If in doubt about how a fabric will fade, make a light fastness test. Take two scraps of the material, pin one to the pane side of a curtain at the window, and place the other in an envelope in a drawer. After a fortnight, inspect them side by side. If there is no difference in colour, you can assume that the light fastness of the fabric is satisfactory. If a difference shows – well, you must make up your own mind, but it can be very disappointing to find that after a few months something you spent a great deal of time and effort over has faded to the point where you have lost the whole effect you laboured to achieve.

It is, of course, quite possible to use other materials, but each will present its own difficulties, and unless you are striving for a particular effect, it is best to stick to firmly woven cotton.

The thread used to join the pieces should also be made of cotton. It is tempting to use synthetic threads, as they are readily available in a vast range of colours, but the effect of using an iron hot enough for cotton on a piece of patchwork which has been sewn with synthetic thread can be disastrous. The resulting ugly brown glob of melted synthetic is just about impossible to remove. The golden rule is to keep fibres and weights of fabric constant in any one patchwork article – cotton with cotton, silk with silk, wool with wool, and so on.

In addition to plain coloured fabrics, begin to collect small prints in favorite colour combinations. Fabrics which are marketed especially for patchwork tend to be very expensive, and are not necessarily more suitable than a lucky discovery on a market

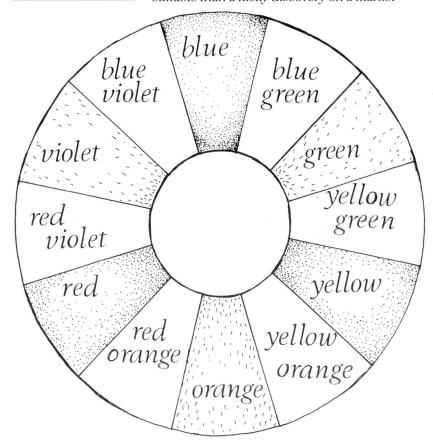

4. Colour wheel

stall. Should you become a patchwork addict, you will experience a storage problem before very long, as you will find yourself unable to pass up any chance to acquire a desirable fabric which could, some day, be useful!

Colour, unless you have some experience of using it in another craft, can cause a lot of anxiety. It is worthwhile to make up a colour wheel (fig 4) and keep it as a basic reference, building up your colour schemes by using complementary colours (i.e. opposite each other on the wheel). A pleasing colour scheme might be made up by using three shades of one colour with contrast given by a little of the complementary. Try, for instance, three shades of lilac pink with a contrast of yellow-green.

The answer seems to be to have plenty of fabrics to choose from, and, if in doubt, to make up a small sample using the dubious fabrics. Often, even experienced patchworkers with good colour sense find that fabrics which seem perfectly usable in the piece are wrong when made up together. Colour Plate 00 shows how startling the use of different colours can affect a simple pattern, in this case 'Farmer's Daughter'.

Equipment

The basic equipment for patchwork is neither extensive nor costly. Most dressmakers will have most of it already. You will need the following:

Scissors
Dressmaking shears
Embroidery scissors for fine work
Paper cutting scissors for paper and plastic

Needles
Sharps and Betweens, the finer the better (The Sharps are for general sewing, the shorter Betweens for quilting).

Thimble
Even if you have never used one before, it is a necessary tool for quilting, and a great boon for patchwork. Ignore the collector's items, but get one which is a comfortable fit on the second finger of your sewing hand.

Pins
I like to use glass-headed pins, as they are usually very fine and sharp, and are less likely to be left in a piece of work than ordinary dressmakers' pins.

Rulers and tape measures
A ruler should be steel, or at least have a steel edge. A tape measure should be in good condition, not worn nor stretched.

Marking equipment
A quilter's pen is a felt-tipped pen filled with ink which disappears when touched with water. It is very useful, but in some circumstances leaves a brown line, and it is suspected of rotting some fabrics.

Watercolour pencils, used for sketching, can be employed as markers as they come in a wide range of colours and wash out easily.

H to 4H pencils give a fine line which is rather difficult to get rid of, but which is inconspicuous.

Templates
Commercial templates, made of metal or plastic, are readily available, and are probably a good buy for a complete beginner, but as you progress you will find that you need non-standard shapes and sizes, so will want to make your own. For this purpose you will need both standard (square) and isometric graph paper (fig 6), sheets of stiff card (cornflake packets will do) or, even better, fine sandpaper or the transparent plastic sheet sold specially for making templates. This has a roughened side which will grip the cloth whilst you are marking, though not so efficiently as sandpaper does. It will, however, keep its corners while sandpaper corners will wear.

In addition to these you will need a good iron and ironing board, supplies of stiff paper (for English patchwork) and, ideally, a sewing machine, although this last is not strictly necessary.

For cutting templates a sturdy craft knife and a cutting board are more effective tools than scissors.

As you progress, you may find you will need some other equipment manufactured for patchworkers, but such items will be

5. *Thimbles*

*Farmer's Daughter'
colour variations*

discussed where they are likely to be necessary as the various types of patchwork are explained.

When you come to make up articles from patchwork you will find you need some kind of quilting frame. Various frames, and their uses, will be discussed in Chapter 2.

Highly desirable, though by no means necessary, is a quiet workroom where work in progress can be kept safe from children, cats, dogs, *et al*, and where your precious dressmaking shears can be kept safe from the younger generation's paper-cutting sprees.

*6. Isometric and square
graph paper*

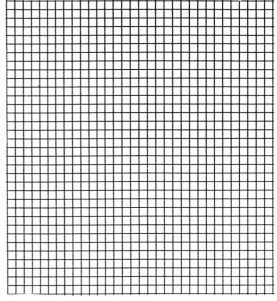

CHAPTER 2

AMERICAN *or* SEAMED PATCHWORK

There are three main methods of making a decorative fabric using patchwork techniques. These are known by many different names, but the commonest terms used are 'American or seamed patchwork', 'English or mosaic patchwork', and 'appliqué'.

Children who are taught patchwork in the USA or Canada will most likely learn the 'American' method, whilst their contemporaries in England are almost certain to be taught to tack their patches over papers before joining them together. The 'American' method is quick, and lends itself to use both by hand and by machine, so I will describe it first.

Double Pinwheel (fig 7) is a 'four block' design – the four quarters are identical, but are set together pivoted on the centre to make the design. Only two templates are required.

The size of the block depends on the use to which it will be put. If it is to be a cushion cover, the finished size could be 38 cm (15 in) square. If it is to be a quilt block it could be anything from 20.5 cm (8 in) to 30.5 cm (12 in).

METHOD

1. Draw out the finished size, making sure it is a true square. Divide this shape equally into four, and then draw in the diagonals to make up the pattern.

2. Cut out the two template pieces very carefully, using a craft knife and a steel rule rather than scissors, and glue them to the smooth side of a piece of sandpaper or a piece of template plastic.

If you intend to sew the patchwork entirely by hand, cut the sandpaper or plastic exactly to the size of the paper shapes. This is because you will need the template to mark the sewing line. Extra fabric will need to be allowed outside this line for turnings. If you intend to work by machine, add seam allowances of 6 mm ($\frac{1}{4}$ in) all round your template. It can be useful to make up the 'patch plus allowances' template as a window template. To do this, cut the seam allowance only from the paper and glue it onto patchwork plastic.

It will be easier to line up the patches for sewing if you cut off the points of the template 6 mm ($\frac{1}{4}$ in) from the points of the patch. A window template will not only allow you to pick out motifs in the fabric, and more easily

line up on checks or stripes, but it is a quick reminder that this is a patch plus allowance template. Write on it what the template is, i.e. double pinwheel, $\frac{1}{2}$ (double pinwheel, template 1 of 2).

3 Templates completed, choose the fabrics. These should be two patterned and one plain dress-weight cottons in toning colours, but contrasting sufficiently for the design to stand out.

4 Mark out the patches on the wrong side of the fabric. The patch-sized template (A) should be positioned so that there is room for two

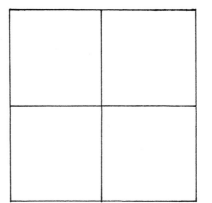 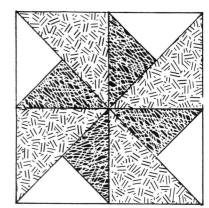

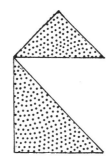

7. *'Double Pinwheel' quilt block*

seam allowances between adjacent patches. The window templates (B) (patch plus seam allowance templates) will allow the patches marked out to touch.

Make sure that the long sides of the small triangles lie on the straight grain of the fabric, but the long side of the large template should be placed on the bias. This will ensure that all the grain lines lie in the same direction and that puckering and bagging are minimized. Do not include the selvage in the shape cut-out.

Mark the outlines of the templates as accurately as possible, using a quilter's pen or a sharp H pencil, and cut out carefully using sharp scissors.

SEWING BY HAND

1 Place the patches together, right sides facing. Using pins, match up the ends of the sewing lines to be joined. Add another pin through both lines in the centre.

2 Stitch the patches together using a Sharps needle, size 8, 9 or 10, and a strong cotton thread. Anchor the thread with two or three

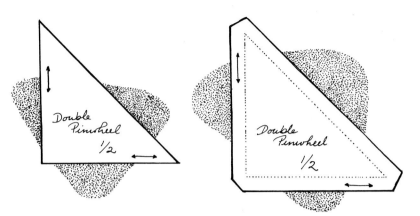

8. Two types of
templates

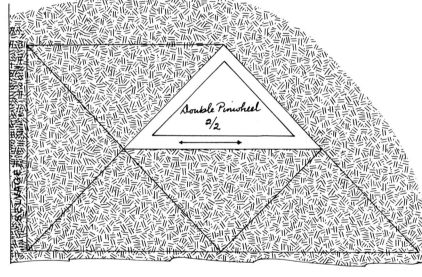

9. Window template in
use

10. Methods of marking
out

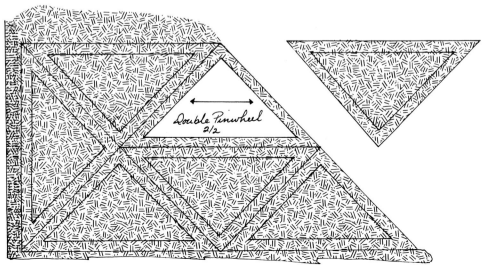

backstitches, instead of a knot, and sew down the line with a fine running stitch (I was taught 'two runs and a backstitch', but my Grannie was a perfectionist). Anchor the end of the stitching with two more backstitches.

3 Have your iron and ironing board within reach and press each seam as you complete it. The general rule is to press toward the patch least likely to show a shadow – i.e. the lightest colour.

4 Always join the small units of a block together first, then join these to the units of the next size, so long as you can work in a straight line. When you have finished matching the triangles, join the four squares together to complete the block.

SEWING BY MACHINE

1 If your sewing machine does not have guidelines engraved on the bobbin cover, place a drafting tape guide on the cover 6 mm (¹/₄ in) from the needle.

2 Align the edges of the patches very carefully, and pin to hold in position.

3 Keeping the edges against the guide, machine the pieces together. It will not be necessary to anchor the ends of the machine stitches, as they will be secured by the stitching of the next joined patch.

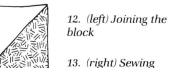

11. *Hand sewing patches*

12. *(left) Joining the block*

13. *(right) Sewing patches by machine*

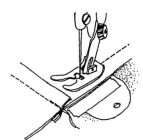

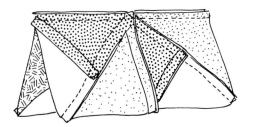

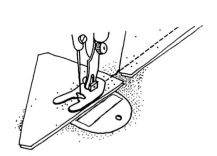

'Circassian Circle' by Gisela Thwaites

Making a quilt

If you want to make your blocks up into a quilt, there are a number of factors you will have to consider. First, you will have to decide what size to make it. In general, mattress sizes are as follows:

King   213 × 183 cm (84 × 72 in)
Queen 203 × 152 cm (80 × 60 in)
Double 190 × 137 cm (75 × 54 in)
Twin   190 × 99 cm (75 × 39 in)
Crib   127 × 68 cm (50 × 27 in)

and the rule for quilts is to allow the size of the top of the mattress plus an overhang at the foot and sides of the bed of 30.5 cm (12 in). This would make a double bed quilt work out at 220.5 × 198 cm (87 × 78 in).

A deep mattress will require a deeper overhang, and styles of treatment of pillows differ. The best method is to spread a sheet over the bed for which the quilt is being designed, and calculate the ideal size from that.

A quilt for a four-poster bed will need a shape that allows for some method of fitting around the bedposts at the foot as shown in fig 14a. An optional wedge can be inserted to accommodate the pillows.

Where a quilt reaches right to the floor, it is advisable to round off the corners so that the corner does not trail on the carpet, endangering the unwary. Fig 14b shows the problem and two possible solutions.

The next decision is the method of 'setting' the blocks. 'Butting', where the blocks are placed in direct contact with each other (fig 15a) takes the most blocks. Another method is to use 'sashing' or 'lattice bands' to divide one block from the next (fig 15b) while pieced blocks may be alternated with plain ones (fig 15c). The blocks may also be set on the diagonal using any of these methods (fig 15d).

Draw out the quilt to scale on graph paper. It is unlikely that you will find any simple block size which fits comfortably into the quilt size you have chosen, but that is no disadvantage as a border is always desirable. Work out the most comfortable setting for a reasonably sized block, and then design a border to complement the quilt top. Fig 15a and 15c show borders which complement the

Ohio Star block used for those quilts.

If you are a mathematician, working out fabric requirements can be an interesting exercise. If, like me, your mind turns to an amorphous jelly if presented with a mathematical problem more complicated than the nine times table, lay out your templates for one block on fabric, allowing for seams, and measure the amount required for each colour. Multiply the figures you arrive at by the number of blocks and round up to the next third of a yard or quarter of a metre for luck.

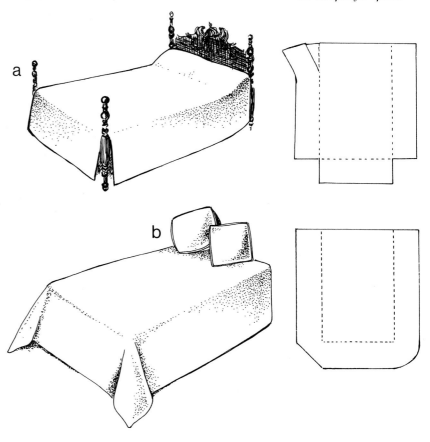

14. Shapes for quilts

Most 'American' blocks are based on grids achieved by folding squares of paper or cloth into the required number of squares and then subdividing these squares to make the patterns. The simplest grid is the 'four patch' giving patterns like those shown in fig 16. The most common basic grid is the three or nine patch (fig 17), but five patch grids (fig 18) provide more complicated patterns.

a.

b.

c.

d.

15. *Setting blocks. 'Ohio Star' quilt block*

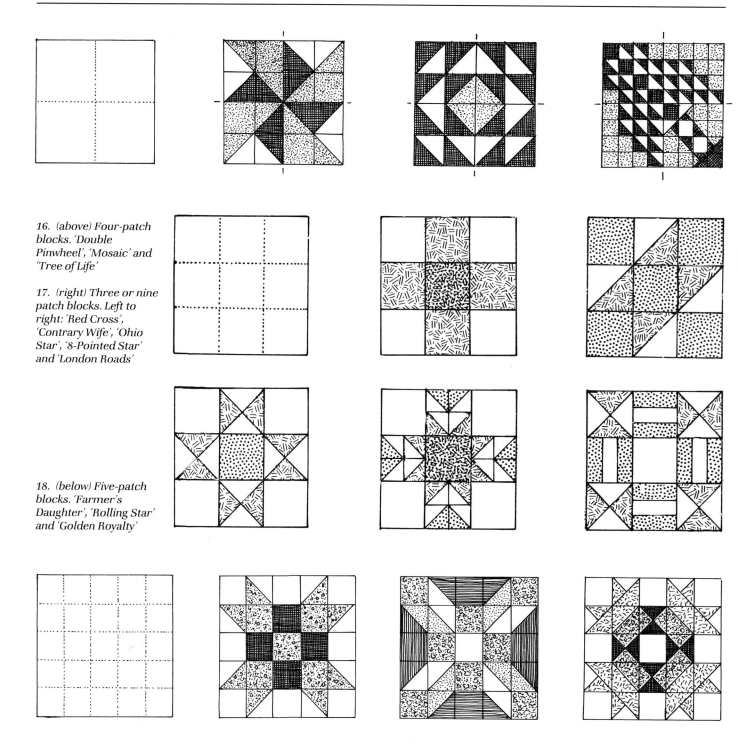

16. (above) Four-patch blocks. 'Double Pinwheel', 'Mosaic' and 'Tree of Life'

17. (right) Three or nine patch blocks. Left to right: 'Red Cross', 'Contrary Wife', 'Ohio Star', '8-Pointed Star' and 'London Roads'

18. (below) Five-patch blocks. 'Farmer's Daughter', 'Rolling Star' and 'Golden Royalty'

Still more complicated patterns are arrived at by butting different colourways of similar blocks (fig 19), or by butting two different blocks to make a pattern (fig 20), but in each case the construction method is the same.

When assembling the blocks into a quilt top, join them into horizontal or vertical rows, and then join the rows, thus avoiding possible problems with corners. Fig 21a shows the assembly for a latticed quilt.

Fig 21b illustrates the assembly for a butted quilt set on the diagonal. Here it will be necessary to cut triangular blocks to complete the edges. Do ensure that the sides of these triangles which will lie along the edge of the quilt are cut on the straight grain, the bias edges facing the blocks. This way you will avoid the possibility of the bias stretching and will not have problems with a wavy edge to contend with when the quilt is being made up.

19. *Designs achieved by butting different colourways of similar blocks*

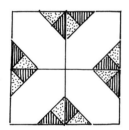
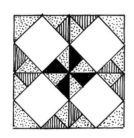
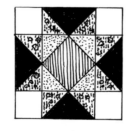
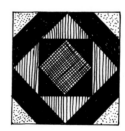

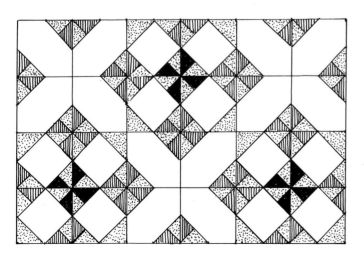

20. *Designs achieved by butting two different blocks*

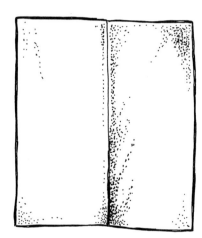

21. *Assembly of blocks for a quilt*

QUILTING

Although there is not enough space in this book to go into the subject of quilting in all its aspects, 'a quilt is not a quilt until it's quilted'!

In English quilting three layers are joined securely – the top, the wadding or batting, and the backing fabric. These are stitched together so that the centre layer remains in position when the quilt is in use and will not bunch nor ball. Making a virtue of necessity, the stitching is worked in such a way that patterns are formed all over the surface of the quilt, either to accentuate the pattern of the top, or to form an independent pattern. Too much stitching will flatten the quilt and make it less warm by decreasing the amount of insulating air held in the layers.

Traditionally, wadding was made from carded raw cotton or from woollen fleece. Today it is much more usual to use synthetic fibre batting which combines the air-retaining 'loft' of the natural fibres with the washability they do not possess, as both cotton and wool will felt if not laundered with exquisite care. An added blessing is that it is possible to purchase quilt-sized batts in one piece, eliminating the problems inherent in joining in the centre of a quilt. It is also possible to obtain various thicknesses of batting.

Backing material for a quilt should, ideally, be in one piece. If it is not possible to obtain a piece of fabric large enough to make the whole backing for the quilt, be sure that the joins are symmetrical.

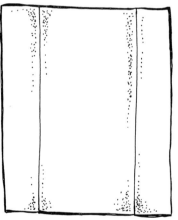

ASSEMBLING A QUILT

1 On a flat surface large enough to spread it out and smooth all wrinkles away, lay the backing fabric, right side down. Anchor it with weights (or by pinning it to the living-room carpet!). Arrange the batting on top, making sure that it lies evenly and is not pulled into thin spots nor bunched. Upon this spread the top, face up. Pin the edges together (preferably with large glass-headed quilting pins).

2 Starting in the centre, tack the quilt together with large stitches through all three layers, the lines of tacking radiating out from the centre.

3 If the quilt is to be quilted in a hoop, it will be necessary to add further rows of stitching to ensure that the layers are not distorted when the hoop is moved.

22. *Symmetrical joining of quilt backing fabrics*

23. Tacking for quilting

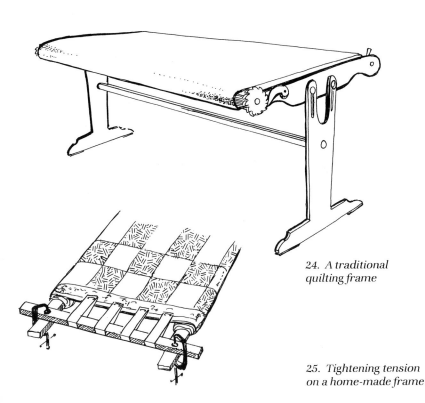

*24. A traditional
quilting frame*

*25. Tightening tension
on a home-made frame*

4 If quilting is to be done in a frame, attach the top and bottom of the quilt to the webbing on the two long bars of the quilting frame – herringbone stitching gives a firm double line – and then roll the ends of the quilt around the bars before putting the cross pieces in place and tightening the tension. To further tighten the tension, attach tapes to the sides of the quilt over the cross bars, fastening them with safety pins as you will need to move them as quilting progresses. Always start quilting from the centre and always slacken off the tension at the end of a quilting session.

5 If you do not have access to a quilting frame, it is possible to use a quilting hoop. These are large, sturdy versions of the embroiderer's tambour hoop, generally 46 cm (18 in) in diameter and 4 cm (1½ in) deep.

Start quilting in the centre of the quilt and work out towards the edges, taking great care each time you move the hoop that both the top and the backing of the quilt are smooth and taut before you start quilting again. To quilt the edges you may need to sew a width of fabric to the quilt in order to hold it securely in the hoop.

6 You can 'quilt in the ditch' (right on the

'Feathered Stars' by Gisela Thwaites

'Rose of Sharon' by Gisela Thwaites

seam line), 'outline quilt' 6 mm (¼ in) from the seam lines, or 'echo quilt' as in Hawaiian quilting (see Chapter 6), but for most other patterns you will need marks on the surface of the fabric to guide you.

For straight line quilting, use narrow masking tape. Place it in position, checking the line with a ruler, quilt along it, and then pull it away. Each piece of tape can be used several times. Leave it in place as short a time as you can, as if it is left on, even overnight, a sticky residue which will catch dirt may remain.

For more intricate quilting, use either a dressmaker's soap marker or a hard (4H or harder) pencil, making a just visible mark on the fabric. The quilter's pen makes life very easy, but it can cause problems on some fabrics, so test each fabric to be used, and leave the mark in place for as short a time as possible, removing the pen line with clean water when you have finished each piece of quilting.

The cleanest method is 'needle marking'. Trace around the quilting template with the point of a needle. The line will remain visible for a short time – long enough to quilt the area. Then mark the next area.

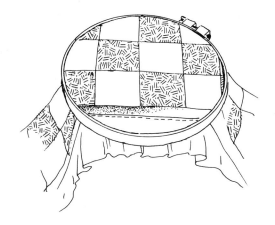

26. Quilting hoop

27. Some quilting patterns

28. Threaded needles for quilting

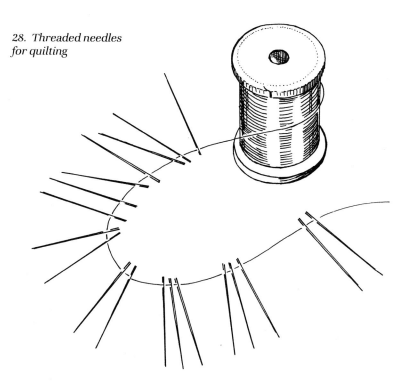

29. Quilting

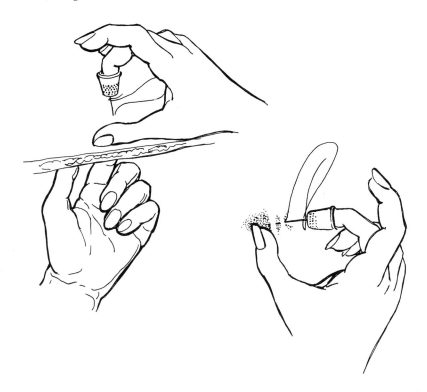

7 The actual quilting is done with a short 'Betweens' needle, size 8 or 9. Sewing cotton No. 40 is an ideal quilting thread. Avoid mercerized cottons such as Sylko, which are weaker.

It is a good plan to thread a whole packet of needles onto the loose end of a reel of cotton before you start, so that as each thread is finished you can take a new one with a minimum of effort. When quilting parallel lines it is a good idea to have several needles in action at once, one in each line, carrying the quilting forward a little way with each in turn.

The usual quilting stitch is running stitch. To start, a knot is made at the end of the cotton and pulled through just sharply enough that it disappears between the layers of the work. A right-handed quilter will hold her left hand under the work to sense where the needle will come through and help it back. Her right thumb will extend to press the fabric down slightly just ahead of where the needle will come up at every stitch. (A left-hander will reverse these positions.) A number of stitches are taken up on the needle before it is pulled through. There is no point in making the stitches very small, so long as they are even.

The last stitch of a needleful of thread must be made secure with a backstitch and the end of the cotton brought out through the top of the quilt, an inch or two away, and cut off short.

FINISHING THE QUILT

There are a number of ways of finishing the edges of a quilt, but three are favourites. The traditional way is to turn in the edges of the top and the backing, enclosing the wadding, and join them with a running stitch close to the edge (fig. 30b).

Equally satisfactory is binding the edge. A matching or contrasting straight grain strip is sewn down to the top edge, through all thicknesses, and then turned over onto the back and hemmed down into the seam line (fig 30a). Some people prefer to use a bias binding made from one of the major fabrics of the quilt.

Small quilts and hangings often have the extra refinement of a piped edge, and this method is also often used when finishing patchwork clothing or cushions (fig. 30c).

30. Edge finishes

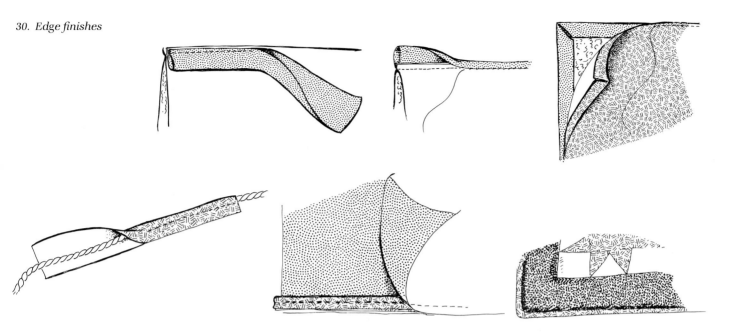

Commercial bias binding can rarely be found in a quality or colour of any use to the quiltmaker, and the quantities required would make it prohibitively expensive. It is much better to take a metre square of one of the fabrics used in the quilt and make your own. Fold the square in half diagonally and crease. Cut notches half way along opposite sides and then cut along the crease line. Join two sides, matching the notches to make a rhomboid, and, using a ruler, draw straight lines parallel to the sloping edges, the width apart being the width required for the bias binding.

Now take the two straight edges (a–b and c–d) and join them, making sure that the seam is the same side of the fabric as the first seam, but offsetting the join by the width of one line. Cut along the ruled line, starting at A, and you will find that you have a continuous strip of bias binding, with all the seams already joined. It's quite magical!

31. Cutting bias binding

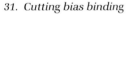

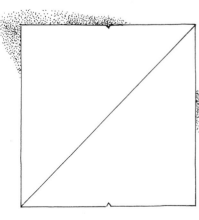

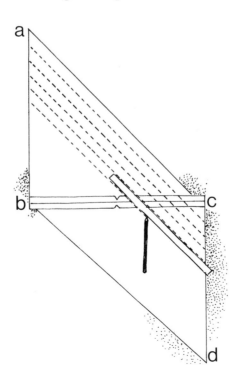

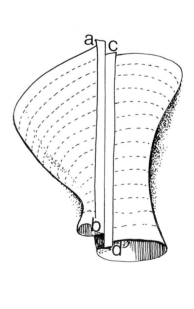

CHAPTER 3

ENGLISH *or* MOSAIC PATCHWORK

When a member of the general public in Great Britain thinks of patchwork and is asked to describe it, the odds are that the type which will spring to mind is one-patch, hexagon patchwork, and there may well be an added embellishment to the description, that it is worked over papers. One such pattern is 'Grandmother's flower garden'.

Grandmother's flower garden

METHOD

To make the basic posy for a 'Grandmother's flower garden' pattern you will need a number of groups of seven hexagons, joined together as shown in fig 33.

1 Either draw out seven hexagons on isometric graph paper and cut out carefully with scissors, or trace around a commercial metal or plastic hexagon template on to cartridge paper, and cut the papers out as accurately as you can.

2 Choose a bright fabric for the centre hexagon and a contrasting fabric for the six surrounding it. Mark hexagons on the back of the appropriate fabrics (one on the centre fabric and six on the other), making sure that two opposing points of the hexagon lie along the grain line. Cut out allowing 6 mm (¼ in) seam allowances all round. A window template, adding the required 6 mm, facilitates this operation. Cut seven hexagons out of the cartridge paper or isometric graph paper.

If the pattern of the fabric is to be an integral part of the design of the rosette, use the window template to select the patch, and join the patches so that the design radiates from the centre, ignoring the grain line in this instance. Cut the fabric hexagons out and pin them firmly to the paper hexagons, checking that the seam allowance is the same all the way round and that the paper is pinned to the wrong side of the fabric.

32. Marking out hexagons

33. (Bottom left) Basic Grandmother's Flower Garden pattern

34. Use of pattern with hexagons

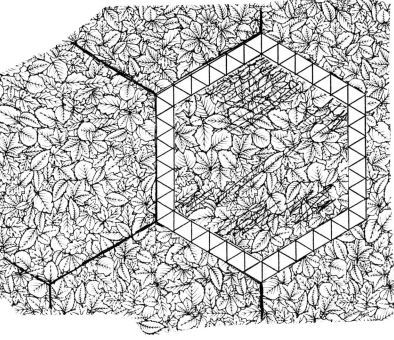

'Grandmother's Flower Garden' cot quilt in Liberty prints

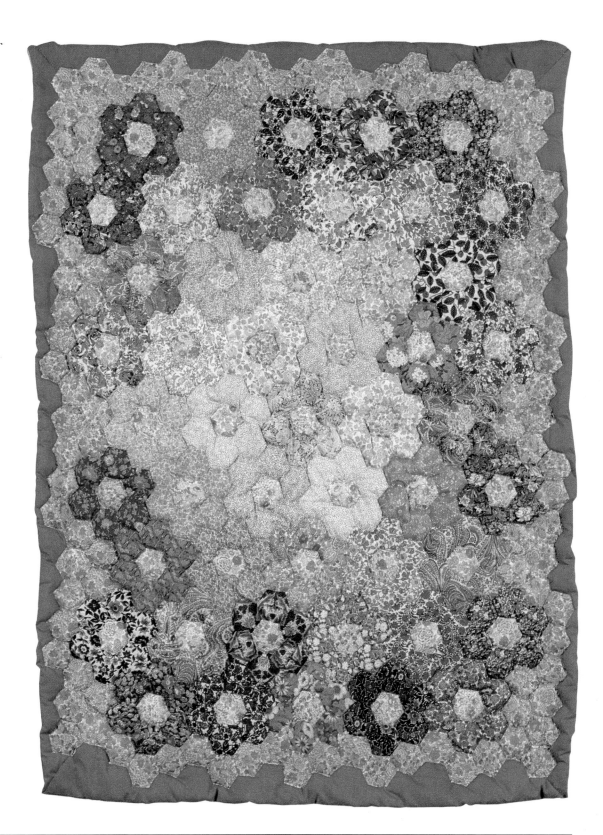

38. Hexagon waistcoat in Laura Ashley fabrics

3 Thread a fine needle (Sharps 8 or 9 if you can manage) with tacking thread and stitch the seam allowance over to the back of the paper hexagon. I like to start with a knot on the *front* of the hexagon and finish with a couple of back stitches – this makes the tacking thread easier to remove when the papers come out. Make sure that the fabric is folded over exactly at the edge of the paper, and that no paper is folded with it. Finish stitching all seven hexagons.

4 Lay the first outside patch on the centre patch, right sides facing, and oversew one edge with tiny stitches, making sure that your

sewing is well anchored with back stitches at both ends of the sewing line. If the sewing is done neatly it should not show on the right side, but try to use a neutral colour of sewing thread in case it does. (It probably will show on first attempts, before one learns to pick up only a thread or two from the edge of the hexagon fabrics.)

Try to avoid stitching into the papers, as, if care is taken, they can be used again and again. When they become crumpled after the second or third use, spray them with water, press with a hot iron, and they will be good for several more sessions.

35. Sewing hexagons

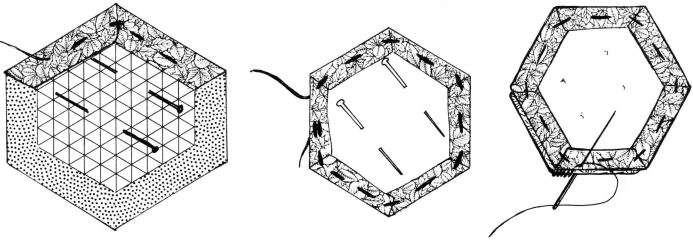
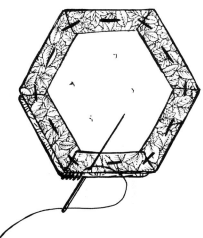

36. Joining rosettes

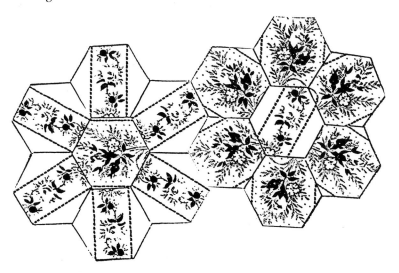

5 Join the other outside patches to the centre hexagon in the same fashion, making sure that the grain lines run on the same line, or that the patches radiate from the centre, whichever is applicable. When this operation is complete, join each outside patch to its neighbour in the same way. Sometimes it is easier to work this stage if the paper is removed from the centre hexagon.

Rosettes can now be joined together directly, or with the addition of further hexagons, to make patterns, some of which are shown in fig 36. When the article is finished, all the paper shapes are removed and the surface of the patchwork checked to make sure that no tacking thread remains.

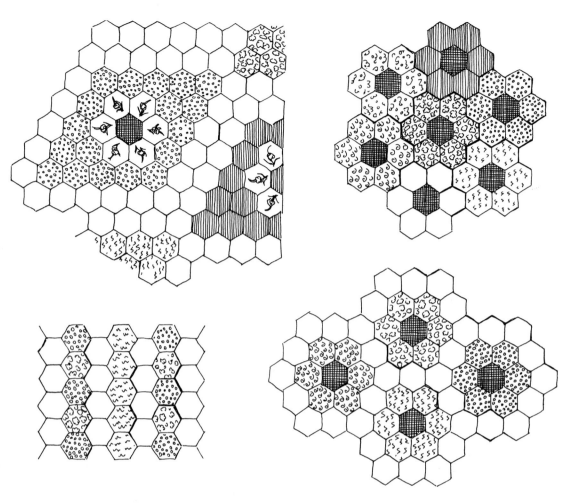

37. Patterns based on hexagons

Cushions made from designs collected from church floors in Venice

Mosaic quilt designed and made by Gisela Thwaites, inspired by Patchwork from Mosaics

Even the most convinced practitioners of the American (seamed) method will be found using the English method for miniature hexagon, diamond and triangle based quilts, as the papers make the joining of bias sides easy, and the jigsaw effect of many tiny patches is easier to achieve this way than by seaming. The extra time taken to cover the papers is more than compensated for by the increased accuracy of the finished product.

The English method is ideal for diamond based patterns such as the star variations in fig 40, but here it is useful to remember not to try to attempt to piece the diamonds together in one go, as this will almost inevitably produce an 'open' centre, but to oversew them together into the two groups of three, then join the two groups with one straight line.

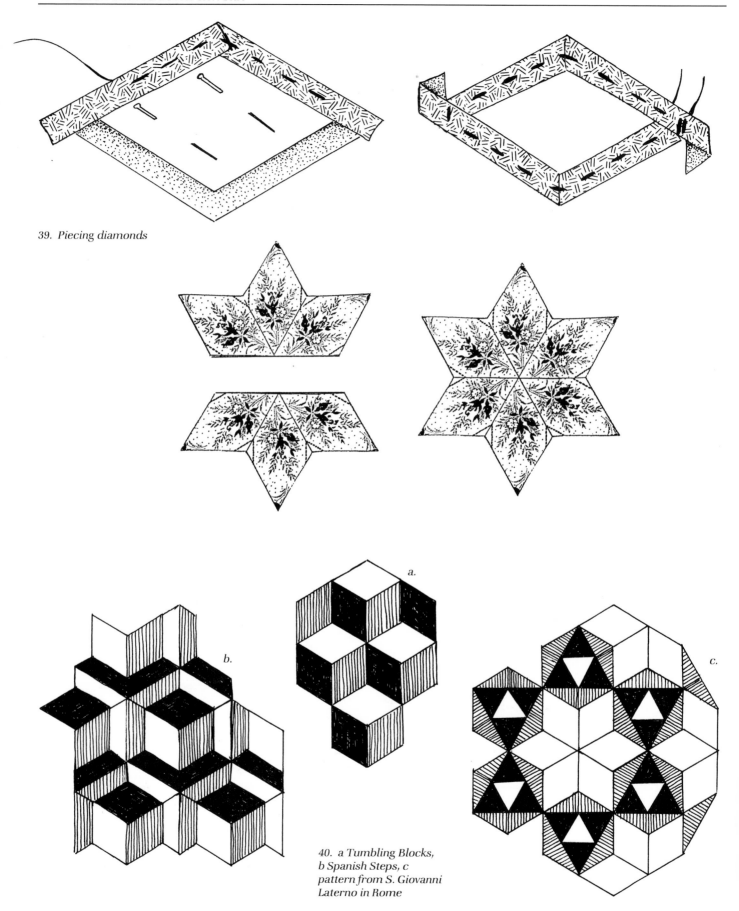

39. *Piecing diamonds*

40. *a Tumbling Blocks,
b Spanish Steps, c
pattern from S. Giovanni
Laterno in Rome*

Mosaic pictures

Although the traditional method of building up patchwork pictures is to use appliqué techniques (see Chapter 6), a really delicate effect can be achieved by means of English patchwork.

METHOD

1 Start with a simple sketch of your subject with colour changes outlined. Overlay with a piece of tracing paper and draw in the main lines with a ruler.

On the tracing paper draw in the construction lines, again using a ruler. If you have an 'inside corner' remember that this is almost impossible to achieve with patchwork, as the fabric will not stretch to make the corner (try it if you don't believe me!), so divide the patch in two.

41. a, b, c (overleaf)
Evolution of Siamese cat
panel

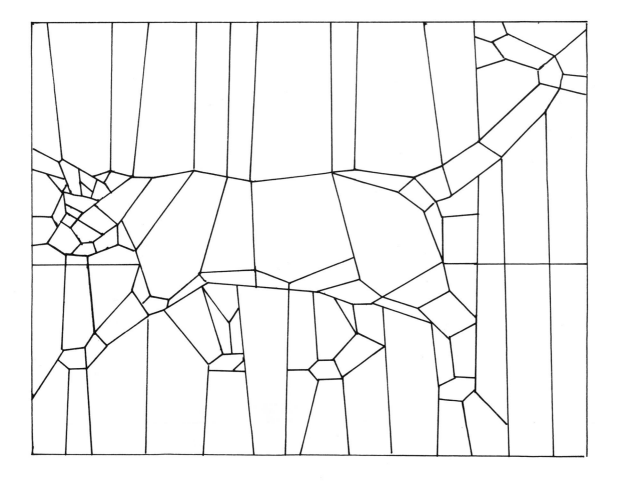

2 When all lines have been drawn in and checked, use two sheets of carbon paper laid back to back between two sheets of cartridge paper. Make sure that the papers are well anchored together before you start the tracing so that the lines are exactly reproduced. Select numbers for the different colours you will use and mark them on the patches (the numbers will be backwards on the top sheet of the cartridge paper, but should be intelligible). The bottom sheet of cartridge paper will be your master copy and should be pinned to pin boarding. The top sheet will be cut up to provide the papers.

3 Where there are a large number of templates (the head, for instance) you will have to allow for the thicknesses of fabric causing distortion, so trim off all trace of the carbon line before you cover the patches.

As each patch is completed, pin it in place on the tracing paper master, and only when all are complete should you join them together, using the oversewing technique described above. If you have been careful, the fabric should have no puckers nor billows when the papers are removed. Press lightly with a damp cloth on the right side.

When I had pieced together my Siamese cat it was obvious that the effect of a twilight hunter was too successful; the cat merged too much with the background, so the outlining backstitch was whipped with a lighter colour before the panel was backed and mounted.

Siamese Cat

Mounting a panel

A panel or wall hanging can be constructed and quilted just as you would proceed for a quilt, but extra care must be taken when putting it together to ensure that the tension on back and front is equal, otherwise you may find in a month or two that the hanging has sagged. To be on the safe side, ensure that, if anything, the back is looser than the front so that any sagging will not be visible.

The easiest way to ensure that the top line of the panel is level is to construct a sleeve wide enough to take a wooden lath which should be just shorter than the length of the top, and strong enough to take the weight of the panel without buckling. Curtain rings can be sewn at the ends of the sleeve, which will fit over picture hooks on the wall. (Similar sleeves are fixed to quilts for exhibition, but should be at least three inches deep).

An alternate method of display for a hanging is to fix loops of the material used for binding the panel between the top and backing. These loops are then threaded over a wooden bar which is suspended on a cord.

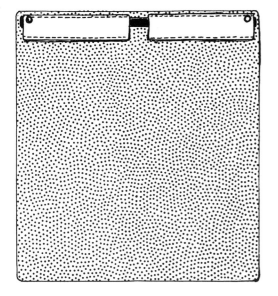

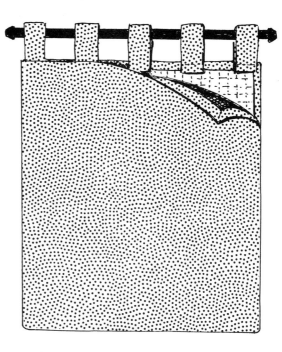

42. *Methods of displaying hangings*

CHAPTER 4

STRIP *and* STRING PATCHWORK

Strip patchwork can be defined as any kind of patchwork where the basic fabric shapes are strips, either in one piece, or a strip made up of several pieces.

String patchwork is Strip Patchwork made up of narrow strips (strings), often scraps left over from dressmaking.

The best known strip patchwork is 'Log Cabin'. This pattern is found on some of the oldest surviving quilts, and its origin is lost, though Janet Rea (see Further Reading) suggests that it may be based on the communal field layouts which prevailed in Britain from Roman times to the eighteenth century. The suggestion that it was based on shadows round a fire is a much later fancy.

There are two basic methods of construction, one employing a backing fabric, and the second where the patches are sewn to

43. Rotary cutter and self-healing cutting board

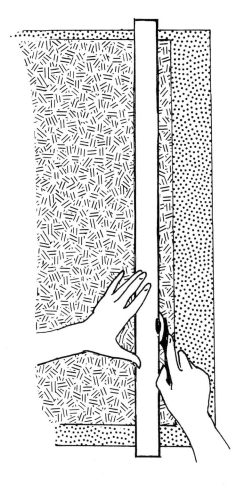

each other by machine without the use of a backing.

Before you embark on either method, go through your boxes of scraps and sort fabrics into two piles. These can be either light and dark (preferably shades of one colour) or graduated shades of two colours (e.g. beige and blue).

Decide how wide your bands will be and then cut along the grain into lengths the width of the finished strip plus seam allowances of 6 mm (¹/₄ in) along each side. At this stage the length of the strip is immaterial. Press the fabric before marking and cutting.

I find it useful to employ a card or plastic template, made as long as possible, and to mark each strip with a quilter's pencil or white marking pencil before cutting with dressmaker's shears. Do not tear the fabric, no matter how strong the temptation, as tearing will distort the weave and no amount of pressing will restore it.

If you are going to make a Log Cabin quilt it might be worthwhile to invest in a rotary cutter and a self-healing cutting board which will cope with several layers of fabric at once and ease considerably the chore of cutting the many, many strips you will need.

Pin your bundles of strips of individual colours to a board so they are readily to hand.

METHOD ONE

1 Select a fabric for the centre square. This may be a solid colour, or you may wish to use the pattern of a particular print. Cut the number of squares you require, the size of the finished square plus turnings all round.

2. Prepare a square of lining fabric (soft, old sheeting will do) the size of the finished block plus seam allowances. Fold this in half diagonally, marking the fold line with a quilter's pen if the fabric will not retain the crease.

3 Pin the centre square to the centre of the backing block, making sure that the sides of the square are parallel to the edges of the block and the corners aligned on the diagonal creases.

4 Take the lightest of the beige strips and lay it, face down, on the central square, making sure that the right hand edges are lined up.

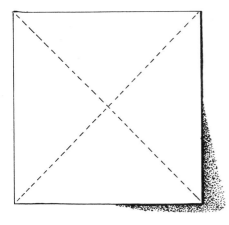
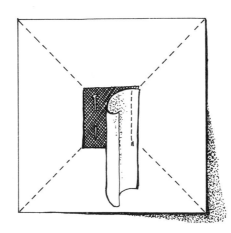
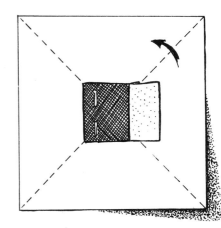

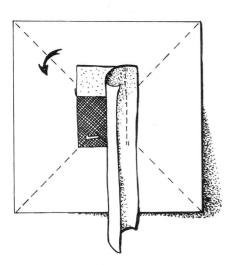
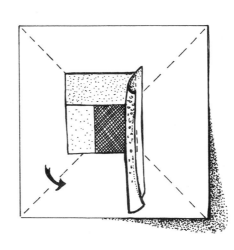

44. Traditional method of assembling Log Cabin block

Log Cabin variation

Stitch a straight line (by hand or machine) 6 mm (1/4 mm) in from this edge. Cut off the excess beige material and press the remainder of the strip over onto the backing block. Rotate the block a quarter turn, counter clockwise.

5 Take the second lightest beige strip and lay it along the edge formed by the first two fabrics. Stitch, trim and press, then rotate as before.

6 Continue with the lightest blue strip, then the second lightest. The fifth and sixth strips will be deeper beiges, the seventh and eighth deeper blues. Continue until you reach the edges of the block with your pressed over strips.

7 Set this block aside and make the others to match.

METHOD TWO

1 Select the fabrics as before, but this time prepare a strip of fabric for the centre square, and machine that strip to the palest beige strip. Cut the resulting double strip to make squares of the centre fabric, open and press. Seams should be pressed towards the centre square.

2 Lay the first joined piece on the second beige strip and machine. Cut and press down.

3 Continue with succeeding strips until you have reached the required size for a block.

You will note that you will need much more of the outside colours than you will of the inner ones. The easiest way to calculate how much of each you will need is to measure the amounts required for the first block and multiply by the number of blocks. This will give you a basis on which to calculate the required yardage for each colour.

There are a number of methods of joining Log Cabin blocks, four of which are shown in fig 46.

There are also a number of variations on the Log Cabin block, a few of which are illustrated in fig 47.

Whilst Log Cabin patchwork is usually made up into quilts or hangings, it can also be used for clothing and accessories.

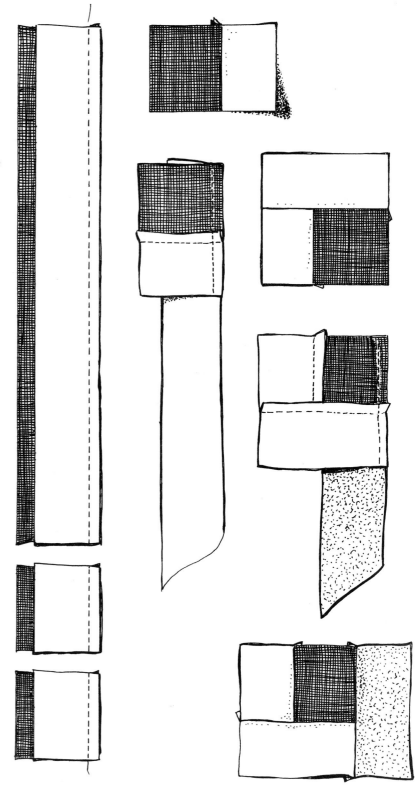

45. Strip patchwork method of assembling Log Cabin block

46. *Joining Log Cabin blocks*

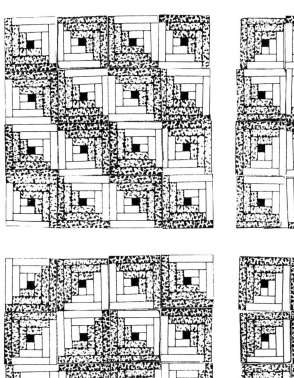

47. *Variations on the Log Cabin block, a – Off centre, b & c – Chimneys and Cornerstones, d – Off-Centre Spiral, e – Courthouse Steps, f – Pineapple*

a.

b.

c.

d.

e.

f.

Log cabin jacket

48. Log cabin tie

Strip patchwork with paper

A somewhat similar method used for other patterns of strip patchwork entails the sewing together of successive strings (narrow strips) of fabric on a base to form a new striped fabric. The base may be another piece of fabric, or a piece of paper (plain newsprint is ideal). The backing fabric will be concealed within the quilt, whilst the paper will be torn off before the quilt is assembled.

Although it is possible to use printed newspaper for the backing, you run the risk of the print being transferred to your patchwork when pressing, so it is better to use the unprinted off-white paper if it is available. Try several papers till you find the weight which suits you.

Whilst it can be worked by hand, this is a technique best suited to machine sewing. When using the paper backing, a stitch length of 20–25 to the inch will allow the paper to tear away easily when you have finished.

Strip quilt

49. *Assembling strip block*

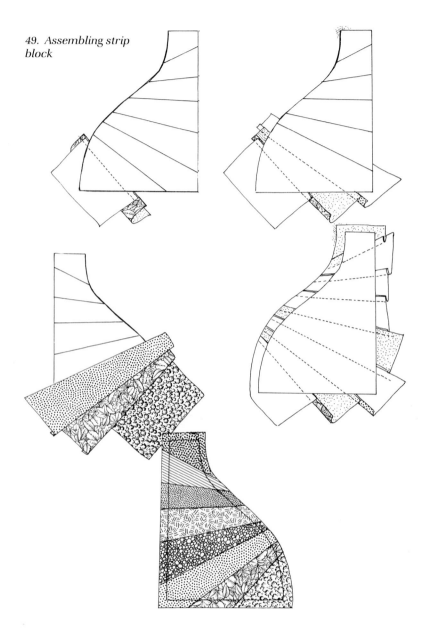

METHOD ONE – *paper on top of the fabric*

1 Draw up your block. Trace the basic pattern on the backing with a carbon paper underneath (a tracing on top of the backing would reverse the finished piece). Cut the sections apart.

2 Lay the first string fabric on top of the second with right sides facing, and top edges lined up. Turn the backing over to show the lines, and place it on top of the 'strings', making sure that at least 6 mm (¹/₄ in) of string 1 shows below and at each side of the backing. Machine along the first traced line.

3 Trim off 6 mm (¹/₄ in) from the seam. Fold the string open and press. It is essential that the fabric is pressed carefully at each stage, otherwise the patchwork will sag or bubble and the seams of the two sections will not meet.

4 Place string 3 under the pattern and under string 2, positioning the top edge about 6 mm above the next marked line. Machine.

5 Continue adding strips until the pattern piece is completely covered. Trim to 6 mm from the paper.

6 Complete the other pattern pieces in the same fashion.

7 Join the pattern pieces by laying the pattern shapes together and sewing along the edges of the backing. You will need to use great care to match up the edges accurately. Tear off the paper, and press.

This method is useful when a pattern demands extremely accurate machining to match up seams as in the examples in fig 50.

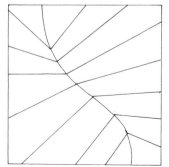

50. *Strip blocks*

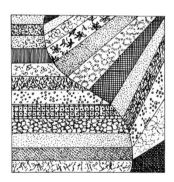

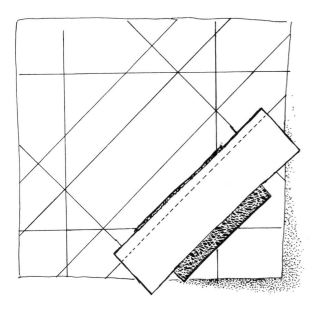

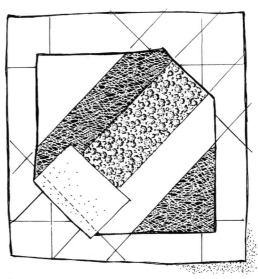

*51. Second method of
assembling blocks*

METHOD TWO

1 Trace the pattern pieces on backing paper. This time the pattern will be traced on the top of the paper, but it will be helpful if the outline of the block is also traced on the back with a second piece of carbon paper. Borders should be left around the pattern pieces so that the sewing lines may be extended.

2 Pin strip 1 to the top corner of the paper pattern, right side up, making sure it overlaps the edges to provide seam allowances. Lay strip 2 on top, face down, matching the edges. Machine. Trim the seam allowance and press open. Continue adding strips until the pattern piece is filled.

Although the seam guidelines are extended on the paper pattern, this method is not as accurate as the last.

3 Pin the completed blocks together, face to face, matching up the corners (this is why you need the tracing on the back of the paper) and then machine along the outline of the block. Tear away the paper.

It is, of course, perfectly possible to make templates for each of the pieces shown in fig 51, and mark and sew without the use of the paper pattern, but it is much more difficult to get a satisfactory result that way.

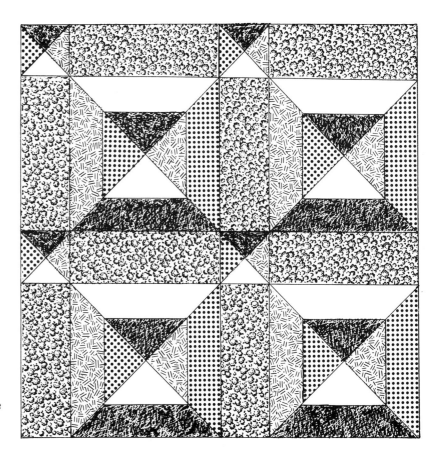

Seminole patchwork

Having acquired sewing machines in the early decades of this century, the Seminole Indians of the Everglades swamps of Southern Florida used them to develop a new type of patchwork. Using strips of fabric in vivid colours, the Indian women constructed patterns which appeared both difficult and intricate to decorate the shirts of their menfolk and their own skirts and blouses. This impression of complexity is very deceptive, for to a competent machinist the method is both quick and easy, as well as being very effective.

METHOD

1 Cut several strips of fabric, as you would for log cabin patchwork, making sure they are all the same width and length. To be traditional, all the strips should be in plain colours, but you may if you wish introduce a printed strip.

2 Lay two strips together, right sides facing, and machine along one edge 6 mm ($^1/_4$ in) from the edge. Open out and press open. Continue until all the strips have been joined and pressed. You should have a length of fabric with the inner strips having a constant width, the two outer ones being that width plus the 6 mm ($^1/_4$ in) turnings.

3 Mark across the width of this striped material with the quilter's pencil, the measurement being the width of the inner strips, plus turnings, and then cut. This will give you a number of small, multicoloured strips.

4 Arrange the small strips so that each row is dropped one square of colour from the preceding one. Line up the joins accurately and machine, using the same seam allowance as before. This strip is now inserted between two lengths of plain fabric at an angle of 45 degrees.

Seminole patchwork cushions in Thai silk

52. Seminole patchwork

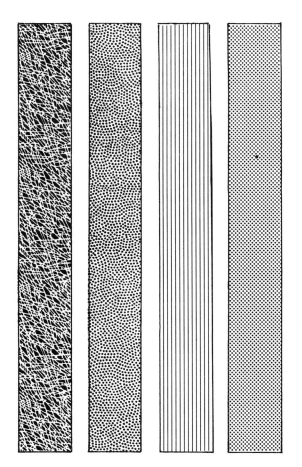

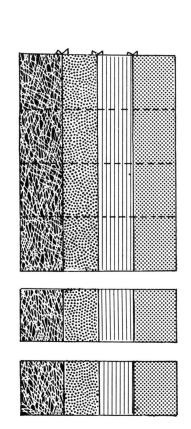

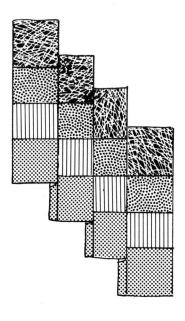

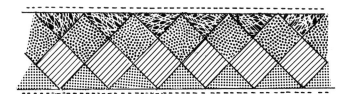

There are many variations on this technique besides the obvious chequerboard pattern. Two basic patterns are achieved by cutting the joined strips at a 45 degree angle. Other patterns can be achieved by combining two or more sets of strips.

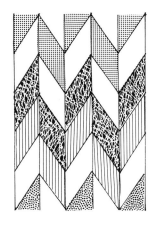
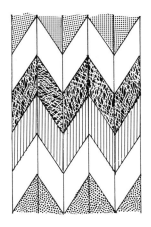

53. *Chequerboard and diamonds*

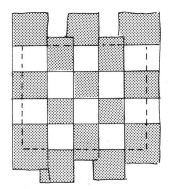

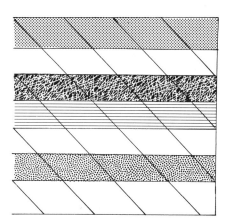

54. *Seminole quilt block*

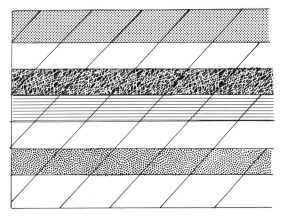

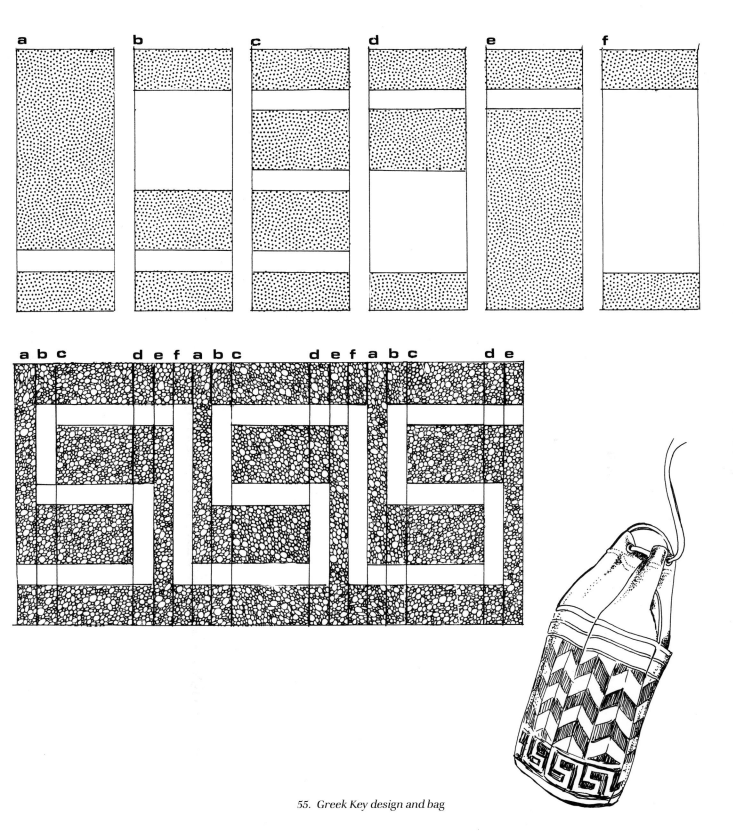

55. *Greek Key design and bag*

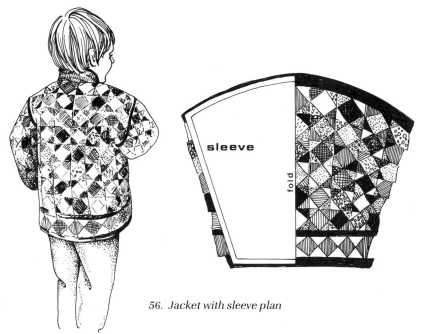

56. Jacket with sleeve plan

Strip and string designs are often utilized for clothing, as they lend themselves happily to this purpose. Be sure to choose a pattern which you know fits (if in doubt, do a trial run with a commercial quilted fabric – it is often necessary to allow more room on underarm seams, for instance). I find it useful to glue the tissue pattern pieces to a sturdy brown packaging paper and cut out. Lay your chosen pattern out on this template to the best possible advantage, varying the size and shape of your design if need be. Make up the piece allowing ample seam allowances, as sometimes the piece will shrink when quilted. Check the piece against the pattern template when the quilting is finished, and mark new seam lines if necessary. When the pieces have been machined together trim the raw edges, but leave enough lining fabric to fold over to make a flat felled seam.

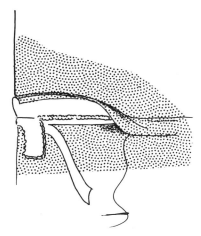

57. Flat felled seam

(left) Seminole quilt by Susan Chastney
(right) 'Dhuri' by Gisela Thwaites

CHAPTER 5

CURVED JOINS

There are a number of patterns which incorporate the use of curved joins without resorting to appliqué techniques. The process is only a little more difficult than those already tackled, and, with care, should present no problems.

The most common designs are those based on a quarter circle within a square. A number of these blocks put together form patterns with such delightful names as 'Drunkard's Path', 'Steeple Chase', and 'Devil's Puzzle', while variations on the theme which turn up in the marble floors of the Baptistry in Florence indicate that since such patterns have been around in stone for at least 800 years, it is possible they have been used in patchwork as long.

a

b

58. Pattern: a 'Drunkard's Path', b 'Steeple Chase' and c 'Devil's Puzzle'

c

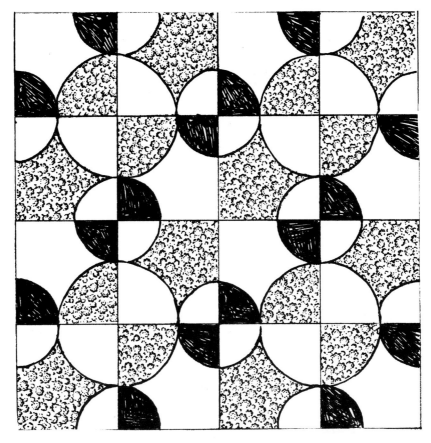

59. Pattern from floor of the Baptistry, Florence

60. Cushion made from pattern in No. 59

METHOD ONE

1 Using the English technique, cut paper templates for the two shapes and cover with fabric by the method shown in Chapter 3. There will be some difficulty in coaxing the fabric around the inside curve, but this may be done by snipping the seam allowance almost to the fold line, and stitching it in place with extra care.

2 Match up the two pieces and pin or tack them together at the centres. Start at one edge and oversew to the centre, easing the shapes to make sure they meet comfortably. When the centre is reached, end the stitching and start again at the other edge. (If you try to work from one side to the other, you will almost certainly find yourself with a bit over – making a ragged join.)

3 Make up all the squares, then join them together to make the pattern.

(right) 'Bottles and Beakers' quilt

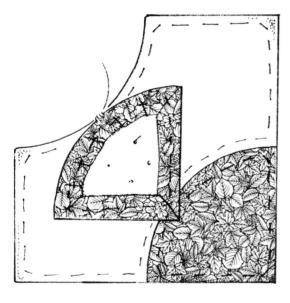

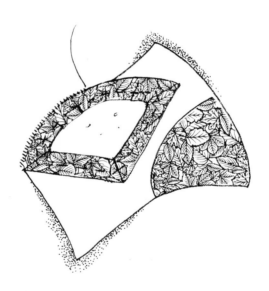

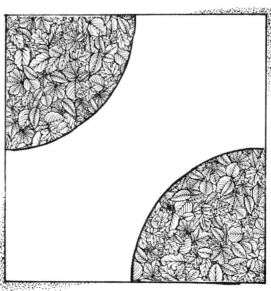

61. *Sewing curved seams by English method*

62. *Marking and cutting patches for American method*

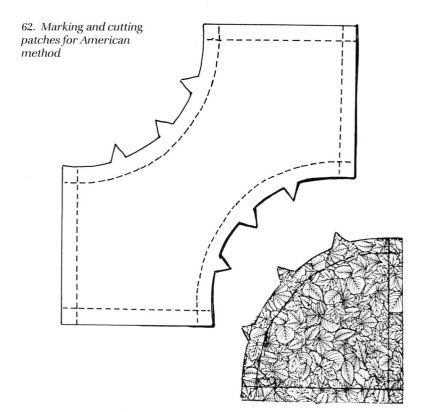

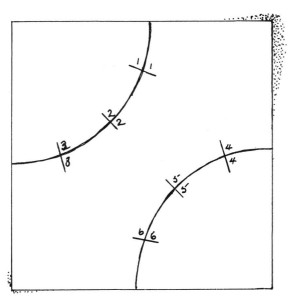

METHOD TWO

1 Draw the pattern on stiff paper or card, marking the balance marks on the curves. The steeper the curves, the more balance marks you will need.

2 Cut out the fabric pieces, allowing 6 mm (¼ in) seam allowances, and transferring the balance marks to the fabric by cutting notches outward from the patch.

3 Lay the right sides of the patches facing each other, and line up the balance marks very carefully. Pin in place. Again sew from the outside edge of the patch to the centre to eliminate the possibility of any overlap.

4 Complete the pattern by sewing the resulting square blocks together.

Either of these techniques may be used to join curved lines in many types of patchwork, for instance the string patterns shown in Chapter 4, fig 50.

The curved seams of 'Bottles and Beakers' provide a very quick pattern to make up, either by hand or machine.

Modified versions of 'Grandmother's Fan' and 'Dresden Plate' can also be made this way, although the strip design of each could also be applied to the background.

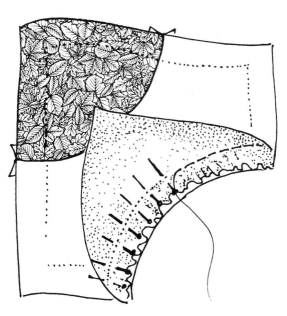

63. *Sewing by American method*

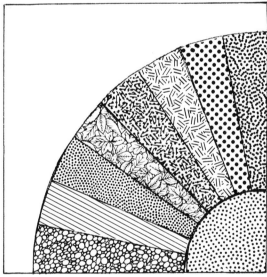

64. (right) Bottles and
Beakers Quilt, detail

65. Modified blocks of a
'Grandmother's Fan'
and 'Dresden Plate'

(left) Grandmother's Fan variation

(right) 'Grandmother's Fan' variation, made from a 35-year accumulation of silk ties

CHAPTER 6

APPLIQUE

Although they are generally termed 'patchwork', the methods described in the preceding chapters should really be called 'pieced work'. Appliqué is true 'patchwork', as the shapes are applied or patched on to a background fabric.

We have no way of knowing how the method evolved. A pretty patch to mend a tear is probably a more likely beginning than the happy discovery that it was quicker and easier to apply a patch of bright cloth to a background than to cover the area laboriously with stitchery, but we will never know which

came first. We do know that the Egyptians used appliqué, and it has been found all over the world, in one form or another, ever since.

The three blocks shown here are classic American appliqué designs. 'Rose of Sharon' and 'Flower Basket' are usually 'sashed' when made up into a quilt, (See Chapter 2) but 'Bridal Wreath' can have the blocks butted to make a secondary pattern at the corners.

67. Appliqué Blocks – a 'Rose of Sharon', b 'Bridal Wreath' and c 'Basket of Flowers'

a.

b.

c.

68. Pattern for 'Hearts and Star' Block

Rules for appliqué

1 The background material should be the same weight as or stronger than the material being applied to it.

2 Edges of applied shapes should be finished in such a way that they cannot fray.

3 Fibres should not be mixed if the finished article is to be cleaned. Keep cottons with cottons, silks with silks.

4 Where possible the grain of the fabric applied should line up with the grain of the background material. This is especially important where the article is not to be quilted, as when the two grains do not match, puckers are almost bound to occur. If the block is to be quilted this may not matter, but it is a good principle to line up the grain lines wherever possible.

METHOD – *Hearts and Star block*

Fig 68 shows a pattern for a cushion cover or quilt block. The squares on the diagram represent 2.5 cm or 1 in, depending upon what paper you use to enlarge it.

1 Draw out the patterns full size on the dressmaker's pattern paper. Draw one heart very carefully, trace it to make a card template, and then use that to draw in the other hearts.

2 Using the card template, cut eight heart shapes out of stiff paper.

3 Cut the background material 2.5 cm (1 in) larger all round than the finished size of the block. Stretch the fabric on a drawing board or table top, and hold it in place with drafting tape, making sure that the corners are square and the warp and weft threads are at right angles to each other. Place your design on this, matching centre and corners,, and pin in place. Using dressmaker's carbon paper, trace the pattern onto the fabric.

Ideally, all grain lines should match, but as it is often desirable to use a 'directional' patterned fabric, it is not possible to stick to this rule. Pin the eight heart templates to the fabric you have chosen for them, and cut out leaving 5 mm ($^3/_{16}$ in) turnings all round. If the pattern is very complicated, it may be useful to make a window template and draw around it on the fabric before cutting out.

4 It will be necessary to get rid of the extra bulk on the outside curves of the patch by cutting little V's almost to the edge of the template. The inside angle is even more difficult, as the fabric will resist taking this shape. Snip almost to the template here, too.

5 Finger press and tack the turnings to the back of the paper template, being particularly careful of the inside angle at the top of the heart. Remove the pins and press the shape with a suitably hot iron (a little spray starch is a good idea). Remove the tacking and the templates.

6 Place the hearts in position on the backing fabric and pin and tack in place, making sure that the patches lie flat on the background. Complete by hemming the hearts to the backing as inconspicuously as possible, using a thread which matches the patch. Remove the tacking.

Because the grain lines don't match up, the hearts will almost certainly pucker. One way around this, which also has the virtue of reducing bulk, is to cut away the background fabric, very carefully, from behind the patches.

With a complicated pattern it may be useful

69. Use of window template

70. Sewing heart shape

to leave the paper template in position until the patch has been hemmed down and the background fabric cut away. With the tacking threads removed the template will pop out easily.

METHOD TWO

1 Where a plain or non-directional printed fabric is used for the patches, a simpler method of working may be used. Trace the design onto the wrong side of the background fabric. Pin a piece of the material chosen for the hearts onto the right side of the block, making sure it covers all the shapes. Tack into position securely by stitching back and forth along the grain lines.

2 Working from the wrong side of the block, machine stitch or backstitch by hand along the traced outlines of the hearts. When all have been completed, remove the tacking threads and cut away the excess material from the front close to the stitched line. Still working from the front, finish the edges of the hearts with machine satin stitch, or with buttonhole stitch worked very closely so that the raw edge and the initial stitching are completely covered.

Use machine embroidery thread for the satin stitching, with normal sewing thread in the bobbin. Match the embroidery thread to the colour of the patch. Make sure that the top tension of the machine is loosened slightly in order that the top thread is pulled through the fabric on both sides of the stitch. It is useful to work a practice piece first to find the width of stitch which best covers the edge.

To start and finish the satin stitches, leave long threads which are later caught through to the back and darned in or tied off.

Always use an embroidery foot for satin stitching: it has a special groove to accommodate the embroidery. A normal sewing foot is likely to jam, producing unsightly lumps in the embroidery.

Machined corners need special care. At the base of the heart stitch level with the point and then, leaving the needle in the fabric, but on the outside of the stitch (away from the heart) turn the material until you can sew away in a straight line. At the dip in the top of the heart leave the needle in the fabric on the inside of the work. If this is not done carefully you will

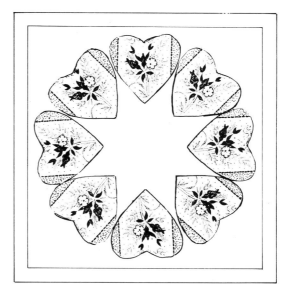

71. *Assembled cushion top*

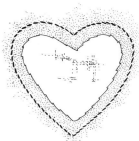

72. *Cutting away back of heart*

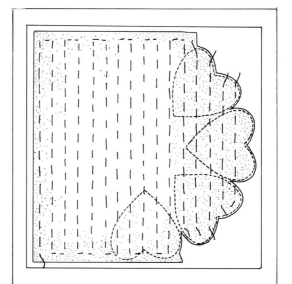

73. *Method of machining pattern*

74. *Covering patch edge by machine. Illustration of embroidery foot*

'Octirine' by Susan Chastney

be left with ugly gaps in the satin stitch.

Handworked buttonhole stitches often look better than machine satin stitch, but the depth of the stitch and the distance between stitches must be constant, or the effect will be untidy.

Some practised patchworkers prefer to cut out the exact shape of the patch and glue it in place with fabric glue before tacking and embroidering it into place. Others iron Bondaweb to the back of the fabric, cut out the shape, peel off the protective backing and then iron the shape onto the block. Experimentation will establish the method which works best for you.

Working a stem

METHOD ONE

A stem, such as that shown in 'Bridal Wreath', is worked by laying a bias strip, folded in half, along the outside line of the stem, and stitching it down either by hand or by machine. The excess material is trimmed away, the bias strip folded over to cover the raw edge, and then hemmed down to the other side of the stem.

METHOD TWO

This first method cannot be used in 'Basket of Flowers' because the bands must be interlaced before they are sewn down.

Take a bias strip and fold it in half as in method one, but machine the length of it, the width of the required band being the distance from the stitch line to the folded edge. Trim off any excess material and press the band so that the seam and trimmed edge are both concealed when the band is hemmed in position.

Pin the basket shape in position and cut the bands to the lengths required. Weave the pattern before pinning,, tacking and hemming the strips in position, their ends being concealed under the edges of the basket shape.

On very curved or looped lines you will find it easier to manipulate the 'stems' if they have been turned out so that the seam is concealed inside the tube.

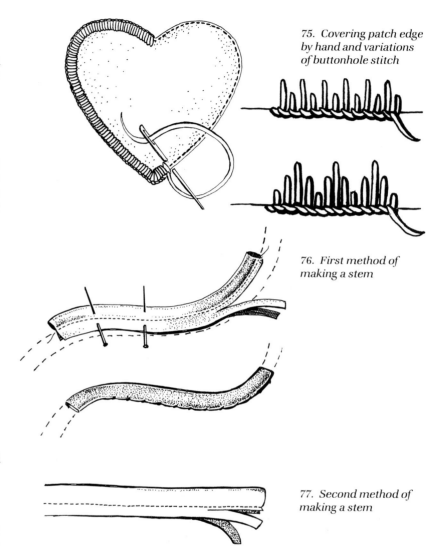

75. *Covering patch edge by hand and variations of buttonhole stitch*

76. *First method of making a stem*

77. *Second method of making a stem*

Overlapping shapes

When working appliqué where one shape overlays another, it is necessary to work from the background forward. Turn under only those edges on a motif which will be exposed in the finished design in order to avoid unnecessary bulk.

When all the appliqué work is finished, remove any remaining tacking threads. Unless the block has become badly wrinkled it is best not to press it, as this will emphasize the turned under edges. Try to press the background and leave the appliqué alone.

Appliqué blocks may be left unquilted, or

have the background lightly quilted in a simple design with the appliqué shapes outlined, either by 'quilting in the ditch' or by stitching just outside the line of the edge of the patch.

When the block is completed it may well have

been pulled out of shape by the appliqué or the quilting, or both. Measure out from the centre and mark new block outlines on the back of the work. The extra allowance on each edge should give ample room to make adjustments.

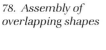

78. Assembly of overlapping shapes

79. (far right) Quilting of 'Hearts and Star' block

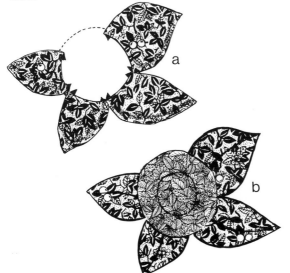

80. Two 'Hearts and Star' cushions

Broderie perse

Until the mid-eighteenth century, when the printing of fabrics from copper plates became common, printed fabrics were expensive and treasured. To make use of small remnants of rare Chintz, Broderie Perse was evolved. A number of motifs, usually flowers or birds, were cut from the remnant and spread out to make a new pattern on an expanse of plain material. These patches were tacked carefully in place, or glued down with flour and water paste, before being embroidered down with fine buttonhole stitch.

METHOD

1 Select a backing material at least as sturdy as the fabric from which the patches are to be cut.

2 Iron Bondaweb to the back of the motifs selected and using fine, sharp scissors and very great care, cut out the patches.

3 Pin out the backing cloth onto a padded table top and place the patches in position, juggling them until you have a pleasing design.

4 Lift off one patch at a time. Peel off the backing paper and replace the patch in position. Using a damp pressing cloth, iron the patch in place with a suitably hot iron.

5 Using not more than two strands of embroidery cotton of a suitable colour, buttonhole the edges very neatly, the stitch being only just deep enough to hold the edges down securely.

Where the pattern of the block does not run into the edge of the shape, or where a wide border can be added to the design, one of the simpler methods of putting a cushion cover together can be used instead of inserting a piping between the back and the front pieces, or sewing them together without a decorative edge. It will be necessary to position the zipped opening away from the edge of the cushion so the backing for the cushion should be cut as a rectangle, the shorter sides being

Broderie Perse cushion with original remnant from which the motifs were taken

81. Cushion fastening

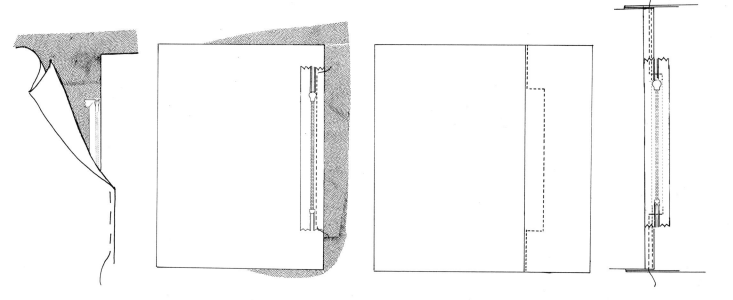

the same as the four sides of the cushion top, the other two sides at least 10 cm (4 in) longer.

Cut this longer piece across at least 15 cm (6 in) from one end. Centre the zip fastener on the cut edge of the longer piece, face down, and sew in place. Now fold over a hem on the shorter piece and sew it down so that the zip fastener is concealed and the two pieces become one again. Place the completed

backing face down on the right side of the cushion top and tack and machine around the edges. Trim the corners and turn out very carefully, making sure that all seams are exactly on the edge. Tack and machine about 12 mm ($\frac{1}{2}$ in) inside the fold all around the cushion top, using a matching thread. This will give a very attractive finish.

82. Selection of flowers for Broderie Perse design

Hawaiian patchwork

The traditional Hawaiian quilt is quite distinctive. The fabrics are limited to two contrasting solid colours, the pattern is a folded paper cut, and the quilting echoes the outline of the appliqué. The quilts are usually square in shape as they were made for decoration, not to be used on beds. A one-piece motif usually covers most of the quilt, although sometimes a border is worked in the same manner.

METHOD – *Snowflake block*

1 Take a sheet of pattern cutting paper or similar 41 cm (16 in) square. Fold this in half and crease it. Make a second fold at right angles to the first in order to establish the centre. With compasses, divide the top half into three equal sections and draw a line along each, through the centre, so that the whole square is divided into six sections. Fold the paper carefully along these lines, and then fold the resulting shapes in half again.

2 Make a paper cut of a snowflake, keeping the outlines simple. Take the fabric from which you are going to cut the pattern, and the larger background fabric, and fold and crease them along the same lines as you did

the paper. Use an iron to make sure that all the folds are distinct.

3 Take one sector of your paper pattern and pin it to the folded pattern fabric through all layers. Cut the fabric carefully through all layers using small, sharp scissors. Remove the pattern. Alternatively, open out the paper pattern and the fabric, and line up centres and fold lines before pinning and cutting out carefully.

4 Lay the pattern fabric on the background, lining up fold lines and centres and, pin in position. Tack with short, firm stitches, 6 mm ($^1/_4$ in) from the cut edges.

5 Blind hem all around the edge with thread which exactly matches the top fabric. Do not cut the fabric to ease round corners, but roll the raw edge of the fabric under with your needle against the line of tacking. This will give you a 3 mm ($^1/_8$ in) turning. Keep the curves as smooth as possible. Turn down outer points to one side, then the tip, then the other side. Because they are not clipped, inner points are always rounded.

When the appliqué is finished, press carefully on the wrong side onto several layers of towel.

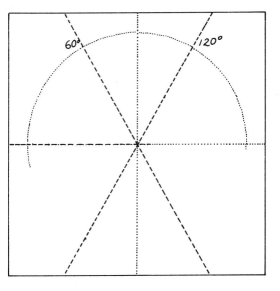

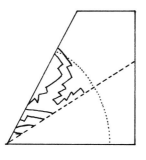

84. *Design of snowflake block*

QUILTING

Sandwich wadding between the top and backing fabric and tack securely in place. The first line of quilting, with thread matching the background fabric, is in the ditch, all around the design. Then quilt echoing lines over the whole surface, in matching threads, creating the wave effect which is so typical of a Hawaiian quilt. The quilting lines should be about 12 mm ($\frac{1}{2}$ in) apart.

Eventually it will not be possible to quilt a complete circuit, but it will be necessary to make up patterns within the spaces left. The simpler snowflake pattern below illustrates the quilting technique.

Do not start out with a quilt for your first attempt. A 23 cm (9 in) or 30.5 cm (12 in) block for a sampler quilt or a 38 cm (15 in) block for a cushion will take you quite long enough. It is not a technique for the hasty!

85. *(left) Quilting of simple snowflake block*

86. *(right) Simple Hawaiian quilt block*

Reverse appliqué: Stained glass patchwork

Reverse appliqué (decoupé) has the main fabric on the surface, the contrasting fabrics showing through from the back.

METHOD ONE

1 Draw out the design, full size, on paper. The 'leadings' – the lines between the colours – should not be less than 1 cm ($^3/_8$ in) wide.

2 Choose a dark coloured fabric, slightly larger than the finished size of the panel. Pin the paper pattern to the fabric, and, using dressmaker's white carbon on *both* sides of the fabric, trace the outlines of the leading. Be very precise.

3 Take the first coloured fabric and lay it on the wrong side of the panel, matching grain lines, and making sure it covers and extends beyond the lines of 'leading' which are to surround the colour. Tack, very securely, through the centre of these leadings, working from the right side.

4 Still working from the right side, using very sharp embroidery scissors, cut about 5 cm ($^3/_{16}$ in) inside the 'leading' lines surrounding the shapes. Work one area at a time. It may be necessary to clip curves and corners to ease the edges under back to the white markings. Blind hem the edges down to the colour, using a thread matching the 'leading' material.

When the areas of the first colour are complete, trim off the excess fabric from the back until the other side of the 'leading' is visible. Continue, colour by colour, until the panel is complete.

METHOD TWO

1 Trace the design, in reverse, on to a medium weight Vilene. Pin and tack this to the wrong side of the dark material used for the 'leading'.

2 Pin and tack the first bright material in place, but this time to the *front* of the 'leading' fabric. Drop the feed of the machine and, using machine embroidery technique, sew from the back along the outline of the 'leading'. To do this accurately takes a little practice, but the stiff vilene will hold the fabric taut enough to work on without a hoop.

When the outline is complete, remove the

87. *Stained glass design from Fawsley Church, Northamptonshire*

88. *Method one of sewing 'stained glass' patchwork. a right side, b reverse*

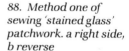

a

b

89. *Second method of sewing 'stained glass' patchwork*

90. (right) Tacking patch for the second method
91. (below) Finishing edges by machine

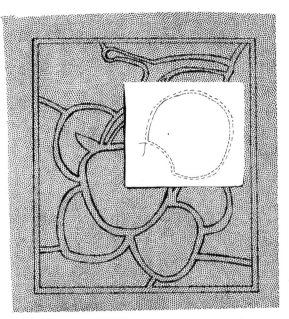

92. (far right) Panel made by variation of third method

Stained glass design from Fawsley Church.

block from the machine and cut away the excess bright material close to the stitching line. Continue with the other fabrics, trimming away excess each time, until the whole area is worked.

3 Lift the feed again. Working from the right side, and using the embroidery foot, machine satin stitch over all the machined lines and raw edges with a thread which exactly matches the 'leading' fabric.

4 If two-ounce wadding is used between the 'leading' and the vilene layers, quilting is done while the pattern is worked.

METHOD THREE

This is similar to the second method, but the bright fabrics are sewn directly onto the vilene, the machine lines being slightly inside the 'leading' lines. When all excess material has been trimmed away the 'leading' areas are covered with bias strips made and laid as shown in figs 76 or 77. This quick method can be quite successful as long as the design is not too complicated.

If a very delicate effect is required, make the traced lines of 'leading' no more than 3 mm (1/8 in) wide and do not lay a 'leading' fabric over the vilene. Instead, when all the colours are laid and the edges trimmed, satin stitch with a dark thread over the rows of stitching with a swing stitch wide enough to cover both rows at once.

San Blas or Kuna Indian patchwork

The Kuna Indians of the San Blas Islands off the coast of Panama have a very distinctive appliqué method. Originally the embroidery was used on Molas – two recantangular panels, front and back, which were joined by side seams and attached to a simple yoke to make a bodice. Gathered sleeves were attached, and the bottom of the bodice had a frill added which enabled it to be tucked into a calf-length wrap around skirt.

This, in essence, is just a more complicated reverse appliqué using three or more layers of fabric.

1 Draw the design carefully on tracing paper.

2 Select and tear (to ensure that the grain lines can be lined up accurately) the layers of cloth. Lay the pieces on top of each other, matching the edges, and tack them together securely around the edges so that there can be no movement.

3 Pin the tracing paper to the top fabric. Using dressmaker's carbon, trace only the lines to be folded to and sewn down on the *top* fabric.

4 Tack firmly 6 mm (¼ in) outside this line and then cut 5 mm (³/₁₆ in) inside the line. Stroke the raw edge under with your needle and blind hem on to the second fabric using a thread to match the top one. Outline all the areas which are left with the top fabric showing.

93. Kuna Indian 'Mola'

5 Place the tracing paper pattern back onto the panel and transfer the outlines of the next shapes on to the second fabric. Proceed as before, hemming with a thread matching the second colour, and exposing the third and final layer.

I find this technique most successful when it is worked in an embroidery frame. Further colours may be added by adding further layers of cloth, or by carefully arranging scraps between the second and third layers.

94. Traditional design, and method of tacking and cutting top colour

Clamshells

This is a very ancient pattern which has been used in patchwork for centuries. It is also one of the very few techniques for which a commercial template is desirable, as most people find the shape difficult to draw accurately.

METHOD

1 Using the metal template, cut several exact copies in light card (postcard weight is ideal).

2 Pin a card template to the *right* side of the chosen fabric, and cut out, allowing 5 mm ($^3/_{16}$ in).

3 Turn the seam allowance on the top curve away from the card. Finger press, and then tack in place *through the two layers of fabric only*. Do not turn under the lower curves, but it can be useful to trace the lines of these curves with a quilter's pen.

4 As each clamshell is completed, remove the template (which can then be reused). Pin the clamshell in place, right side up, on pinboarding. Either use a Macramé board (which has ruled squares as a guide) or pin a piece of elastic securely across your pinboarding to provide a straight line.

5 When all the clamshells required for the design have been completed and pinned into position, tack them in place a row at a time. Whilst it is possible to tack them into position onto a backing sheet of calico, they can just as successfully be sewn on to each other.

6 When the tacking is complete, lift them from the board and blind hem around the patches.

7 It will be necessary to work beyond the edges of the block and trim away excess material when the article is ready to be made up.

There are many satisfactory arrangements of clamshells, and the use of circles extends the possibilities. Quilting, where desired, usually follows the outline of the clamshell.

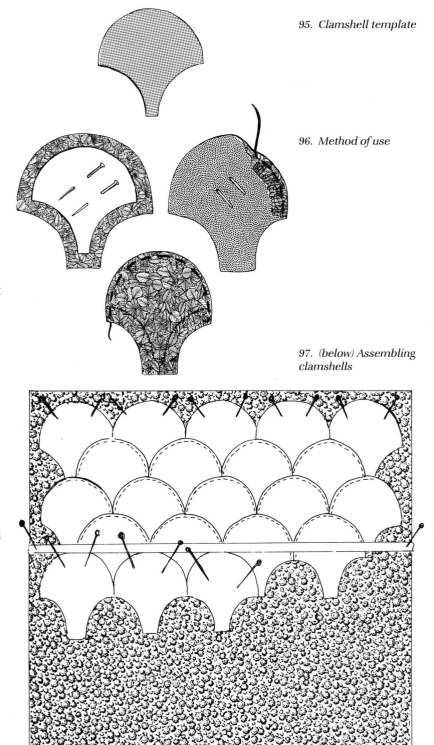

95. Clamshell template

96. Method of use

97. (below) Assembling clamshells

Clamshell cushions in Liberty lawn

(left) 'Kuna' tulips

Crazy patchwork

Although the technique is much older, there was a time, a century ago, when crazy patchwork reached its apogee in America. For 35¢ one could buy a package containing enough pieces, in a variety of colours, to make up a 12 inch block. These packages were silk offcuts which would otherwise have been thrown away.

Crazy patchworks were assembled from collections of scraps of exotic materials, often velvets and brocades, arranged in no formal pattern. The fabrics might be left plain, but were often decorated with embroidery. Women's magazines of the time contained patterns for tracing onto crazy patchwork, and newly introduced iron-on transfers were much in demand for this purpose. By 1900 the fashion had passed, and crazy quilts were out of favour, to be thrown away or tucked away in trunks and drawers, and forgotten.

METHOD ONE – *Victorian style crazy patchwork*

1 Select scraps of material which harmonize with each other in colour and texture. Press them to remove creases.

2 Cut a foundation block of a sturdy cotton fabric, the size of the finished block plus seam allowances. Lay the first patch of fabric to cover one corner of the block. Pin this in place leaving the inner edges free.

3 Select and trim more patches, slipping them under the free edges of the first patch, and pinning them in place. Do not turn the edges under, as these will be covered with embroidery, and any extra layers will cause problems.

4 Repeat the performance until the block is completely covered with fabric.

5 Tack the patches firmly in place and remove the pins. Sew down the edges with running stitches or blind hemming.

6 Now cover the edges with embroidery stitches, using an embroidery thread of a weight to suit the fabrics. In order to create unity in the block it is best to use one colour for the outline stitches, though other colours can be added if individual patches are to be decorated.

Fig 100 shows some stitches commonly used in crazy patchwork.

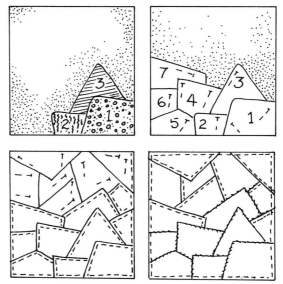

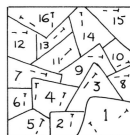

98. *Crazy Patchwork method*

When all the blocks planned for a quilt have been completed, sew them together by butting and seaming them, or by sashing them with strips of velvet or other suitable fabric. Of course, many Victorian quilts were made of one piece and not by assembling individual blocks, but the block method is much the easiest for a beginner.

The quilt should be lined with a fabric compatible with the scraps used on the front. As the top will be heavy it is not usual to have a layer of wadding. Back and front can be fastened together with whipped or stem-stitched 'spiders webs' or tied as shown in Chapter Seven. The edges should be bound.

Lightweight materials (fine silks or cotton lawns) can be assembled in the same way to the tacking stage, but when being sewn down the edges should be stroked under and hemmed so that adequate lapping allowances are necessary. Such patchwork may be left without embroidery if the fabrics are sufficiently interesting.

99. *Finishing edges of silk patchwork*

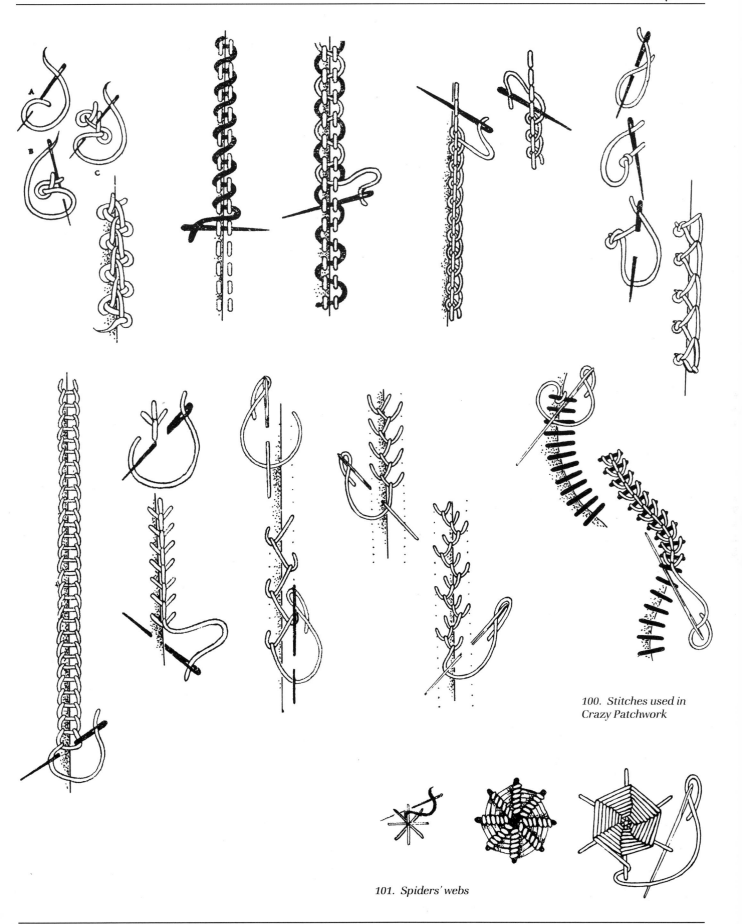

100. Stitches used in
Crazy Patchwork

101. Spiders' webs

METHOD TWO – *quick crazy patchwork by machine*

1 To make the cover for a chair pad by machine, cut two pieces of cotton fabric to the shape and size required for the top and bottom of the chair pad, leaving 2.5 cm (1 in) turnings all round. Place a piece of two-ounce wadding, the same size and shape, onto one pad backing and tack securely in position.

2 Starting in one corner, pin a cotton patch into position. Take a second patch, lay it face down on top of the first, and machine along one side through all thicknesses. Turn the second piece over and pin in the open position.

3 Continue building up with further patches. At first all raw edges will be covered easily, but there will come a time when it is not possible to do this. Turn under the raw edges, pin the patches in place and continue to build up the pattern.

It will have been necessary to plan the whole operation fairly carefully: a pleasing random pattern does not just happen! If a spot is left out, or raw edges are left uncovered, it is easy to cover the fault with a small patch with all its edges turned under.

4 When the whole pad is completely covered with patches, turn the machine controls to an embroidery stitch and oversew all the join lines until each has been secured and embellished. Loose ends are taken through to the back and tied off. The top will have been patched, embroidered, and quilted in two quick operations.

5 Repeat for the bottom shape. Trim both to the correct size and shape, allowing 1.5 cm (⁵⁄₈ in) turnings.

6 To make a gusset, cut a strip the required width, plus turnings, and long enough to go three quarters of the way around the pad. Cut a second strip, at least 2.5 cm (1 in) wider than the first, and a little longer than one quarter the distance around the pad. These two pieces should be padded, patched and quilted.

7 Split the wider piece in half, lengthwise, and machine a zip fastener in position between these two strips. Machine the strip thus formed to the end of the first strip.

8 Tack the gusset in position so that the zip is at the centre back. When you have adjusted the length, undo the tacking a little way and machine the zipped piece to the other end of the gusset. Retack and machine the gusset in place.

9 Fit the bottom pad to the gusset and tack and machine this in place, making sure that the zip-fastener is left partially open, otherwise it will be difficult to turn the finished chair pad cover to the right side.

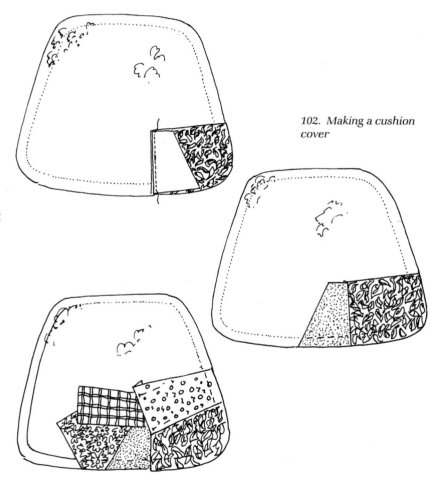

102. *Making a cushion cover*

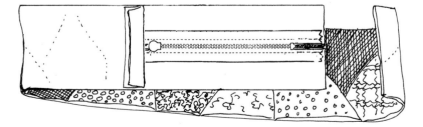

103. *Making the gusset*

Crazy Patchwork quilt made before her marriage by Mary Anne Loman, who died, aged 84, in 1925. It is now in the possession of her nephew's daughter, Joan Adcock, to whom it was given when she was born

CHAPTER 7

OTHER KINDS *of* PATCHWORK

There are several ways that fabric can be manipulated to produce a decorative effect which do not fit into any of the previous chapters, but which, nevertheless, are included under the general heading of patchwork.

The first, puff patches – or biscuit patchwork – is useful as a warm bed covering, but the other three are employed mainly for decoration and, as the processes tend to be tedious, are more usually chosen for small articles instead of for large quilts or wall hangings.

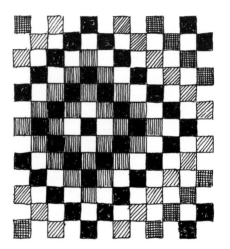

104. 'Triple Irish Chain' and 'Trip Round the World'

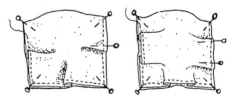

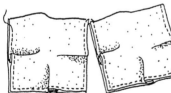

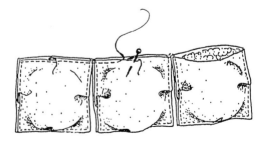

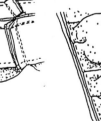

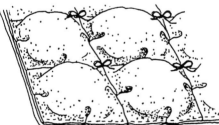

105. Puff or Biscuit patchwork

Puff patches

1 Design your quilt on graph paper – as squares are used throughout, simple cross stitch patterns can be used, or patchwork designs such as 'Irish Chain' and 'Trip Around the World'.

2 Cut the backing squares from muslin, or any other lightweight cotton fabric (it will be completely hidden when the quilt is finished, and is only used to hold the patch in shape). The square should be the finished size of the patch, plus turnings (9 cm for a 7.5 cm patch – $3^1/_2$ in for a 3 in patch).

3 For the top of each puff, cut a square of fabric 1.2 cm to 2.5 cm ($^1/_2$ to 1 in) larger than the base square. The larger the top square, the fuller the puff will be. If desired, the top of the patches can be decorated with embroidery at this stage.

4 With the *wrong* sides of the fabrics together, match the corners of the squares and pin. Pin one or two pleats on each side to make the top square fit the bottom one. Machine sew or backstitch by hand around three sides of the squares. If working by machine, this may be done assembly-line fashion.

5 Stuff each puff with a little fibrefil or wool. Pin pleats on the unsewn edges to match those on the other three sides. Close this side by hand or machine.

6 When all the puffs have been made, lay them out in the pattern you have chosen. Take two adjacent puffs and place them *right* sides together, joining them with a 6 mm ($^1/_4$ in) seam. Continue joining puffs till you have a row right across the quilt. Make the other rows in the same fashion.

7 Join the rows together, folding the seam allowances in opposite directions to make it easier to ensure that the original seams match.

8 Place the completed puff top face up on lining material. Without undue stretching, pin the edges of the puffs and the lining together. Pin at the corners where the puffs join. Tie the puffs and lining together at the corners, removing pins as you go. The edges are finished with binding.

To tie a quilt of any kind you need a larger needle than you would normally use – a Chenille needle with a large eye and a sharp point is ideal – and a string or cord which will hold a knot. Take a stitch or a backstitch through all layers of the quilt, with a doubled thread of your tie and leave ends of at least 2.5 cm (1 in). These are then tied together in a square knot. Ties are made at regular intervals. This is a very much quicker way of finishing a quilt than quilting it, and, if the knots are well made, quite as durable.

106. Tying a quilt

An alternative method of finishing is to lay the puff top on the lining material (which has already been cut to size) with *right* sides together. Pin and tack around the edges, and then machine around three sides, leaving only enough of the fourth side open to allow the quilt to be turned right sides out. When this has been done, close the opening with blind stitch. Tie the top and lining together at the corners as before.

Suffolk puffs

This variation on puff patchwork is made with gathered circles. Although any fabric can be used: the finer and lighter it is, the easier it is to work. Liberty Tana Lawn is an ideal fabric.

It is difficult to establish why these are called 'Suffolk puffs', as they turn up in many other places around the world. My Asian students were quite astonished to find them given an English name, as the method is a traditional one in the Indian subcontinent.

METHOD

1 Using compasses, make a circular template twice the diameter of the finished puff. Cut a number of these circles in the fabric.

2 With a strong sewing thread turn a 6 mm (1/4 in) hem all around the circle. (Fig 107). Make sure the stitches are even, but not too small as too many stitches will give too large a centre hole in the puff. (It is useful to experiment as the size of the stitch and the depth of the turn both depend on the weight of the fabric). Now pull up *both* ends of the sewing thread, easing the fabric so that the gathers are even. Pull up as tightly as you can and knot the two ends of the thread together. Trim, and tuck the ends inside the puff. Treat the other circles in the same fashion.

3 If desired, the puffs can be decorated at this stage. Try inserting a scrap of contrasting fabric inside the puff before pulling it up completely, or sew a fancy button over the opening left by the gathers.

4 Join the puffs together by placing them face to face and catching them together with a few secure oversewing stitches. Spaces may be left, as shown in fig 107, or the puffs may be joined all the way round by pulling them into hexagons.

Suffolk puffs are usually employed solely as decoration, though a summer shawl of puffs, or a pram or cot blanket for very hot weather, would provide a little protection without being too warm. My personal feeling is that this type of 'patchwork' belongs more truly in the category of 'embroidery': depending on the treatment and the fabric used, it makes quite realistic blossoms, and very convincing barnacles!

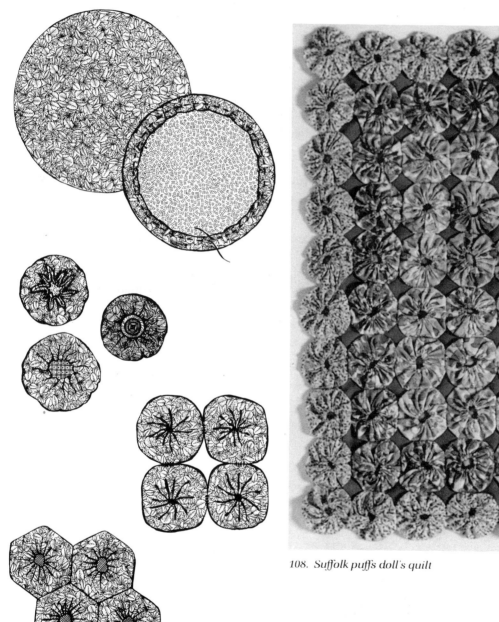

107. *Suffolk puffs*

108. *Suffolk puffs doll's quilt*

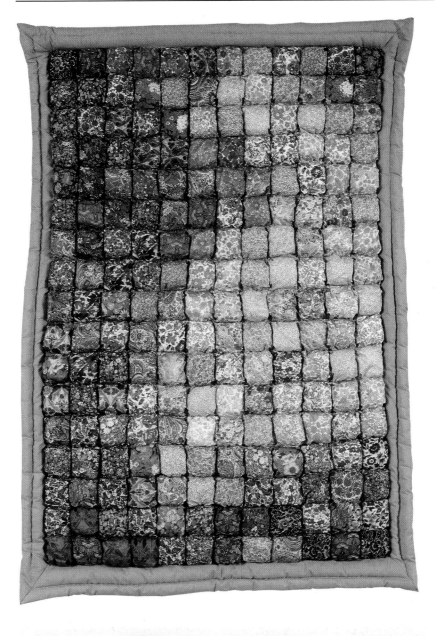

Cathedral window cushions

*Puff or Biscuit
Patchwork quilt in
Liberty lawns*

Cathedral window patchwork

This decorative use of fabric is achieved by folding and refolding foundation shapes of fabric, and decorating them with appliqué in contrasting colours. It is a somewhat laborious process, using rather a lot of fabric, but the finished effect is unique and often very attractive. There are two basic methods, one traditional and a modern, quicker, alternative.

METHOD ONE

1 Cut a 15 cm (6 in) square of the base colour. This fabric should be a firm cotton which will hold a crease. Turn over 3 mm (1/8 in) all round to the wrong side and press.

2 Fold the four corners to meet in the middle and press. Pin firmly in place as shown in fig 109.

3 Fold these four corners to the centre and pin in place as in fig 109. Stitch the points together securely with a matching thread. Do not catch in the underlying fabric. The pins may now be removed.

4 Place two finished squares with right sides facing, and oversew the two edges firmly together along one side, making sure that the points of the corners are securely attached. It may be necessary to tease the shapes a little to make them fit.

5 Cut the squares for the decorative centres of the folded patches. These should be slightly smaller all round than the folded squares, but as this measurement will be governed by the characteristics of both fabrics being used, before cutting the rest of the number required make a trial square to find out the measurement you will need for your particular patch. Pin these squares in position over the seams joining the folded patches.

6 Curl one edge of the base fabric over the edge of the centre patch and sew down with tiny stitches in a matching thread, stab stitching right through to the back of the patch. Continue round each square, making sure that the corners are neat and tidy. This stitching gives the effect of quilting on the back of the patchwork.

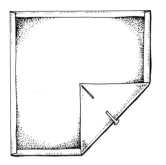

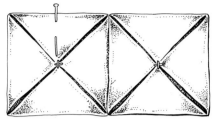

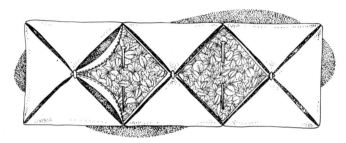

109. *Cathedral window patchwork, method one*

METHOD TWO

1 Cut out the square of base fabric exactly as for method one, but instead of folding over the edges, fold in half with the right side of the fabric inside the fold. Sew up both ends by machine, using 6 mm (¹/₄ in) seams.

2 Press the seams open and fold again so that it is possible to sew the remaining sides together, leaving a space near the centre open to turn the patch through to the right side (fig 110). Clip the corners before turning out.

3 Fold the corners to the centre and press firmly to make a creased line. Open out again and sew to the next patch by matching the creased lines and sewing along them (fig 111). Refold, and stitch the points together at the centre.

4 Add the contrasting patches as shown in method one.

If the fabric used for the backing in method two will not hold a crease, it is advisable to join the patches together as shown in method one.

Method two allows the use of many exotic background fabrics which would be exasperating, if not impossible, to use with the traditional method – for instance, silk jersey, panne velvet, and springy synthetics which will not hold a crease. It may be difficult to achieve a neat centre with such fabrics, in which case the solution is to catch the four points together securely with a matching thread and then, slipping the needle down a fold, catch the two sides of the point together

with oversewing 3 mm (¹/₈ in) to 6 mm (¹/₄ in) from the point.

When estimating the quantity of fabric required for cathedral window patchwork, it is only necessary to remember that you double the length and width of the finished patch and add seam allowances. In fig 112 a–b is the length of the side of the finished folded patch, and is half c–d which is the basic square, less seam allowances.

You may wish to make a panel of different shapes of folded patches, as shown in fig 113.

To establish the basic shape for any rectangle, take the finished patch size (in heavy print in fig 114) and measure the distance from the middle of each side to the centre, extending this measurement outwards. Join the points thus arrived at to make a diamond shape around the centre rectangle. Using compasses based on point a and the length of line ab, describe an arc outside the diamond. Bisect it with another arc (d) with the compasses based on point c and the length cb. Join a–d and cd. Draw similar triangles on the other sides, and then add the seam allowance.

This shape may be put together using either method one or method two.

110. Cathedral window patchwork, method two

a.

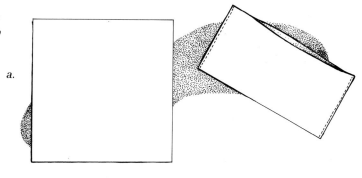

b.

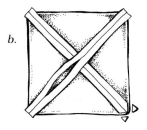

c.

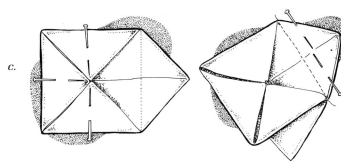

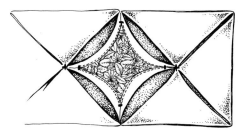

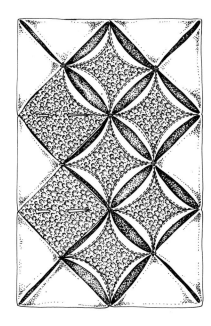

111. Corner treatment

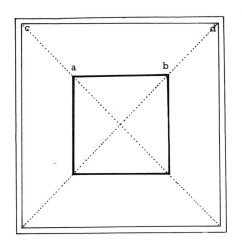

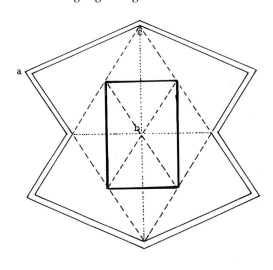

112. Designing the block

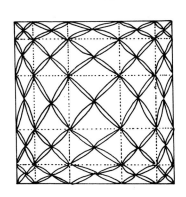

113. Varied sizes of patches

114. Designing oblong block

Folded stars or Somerset patchwork

This technique is really for decoration only, as the stitched points are unlikely to stand up to any real wear.

METHOD

1 Cut a square of backing cotton a little larger than the finished motif – a 15 cm (6 in) block is a good size to start with. Fold, or mark with tacking cotton or a pencil, the lines shown in fig 115.

2 You will need several fabrics in contrasting colours. Patterned fabrics can be used, but must be selected very carefully for effect. Plain cottons are the best choice for a first attempt.

Cut four pieces 6 cm (2½ in) square from the first colour chosen. Fold each of these in half. Fold again so that the corners meet at the centre as in fig 115.

Alternatively, cut four pieces 6 cm × 3.6 cm (2½ in × 1½ in), fold over 6 mm (¼ in) along the top edge, and then fold the corners over as shown in fig 119c. The square makes the work easier in the earlier stages, but the build-up of fabric makes sewing more difficult, and the resulting patchwork bulky and stiffer than the pattern worked by the second method.

3 Place the first triangle on the backing fabric as shown in fig 116. Catch the centre point securely to the backing with two or three stitches through the point, keeping them as invisible as possible. Pin or tack the base of the triangle to the backing material. Complete the first square by positioning and sewing down the other three triangles.

4 For the second row, cut and fold eight pieces of the same size as before, but in a different colour. Place each triangle on one of the radiating lines on the backing fabric. Making sure that all the points are equidistant from the centre, and that the centre lines of the patches lie along the radiating lines, pin or tack and then sew the points down securely, catching the first blocks in place as you do.

5 It may be desirable to increase the number of patches in succeeding rows, depending on how they are arranged. If a circular motif is desired, finish placing patches when the triangles reach the edges of the backing square at the centres of the sides. The backing can

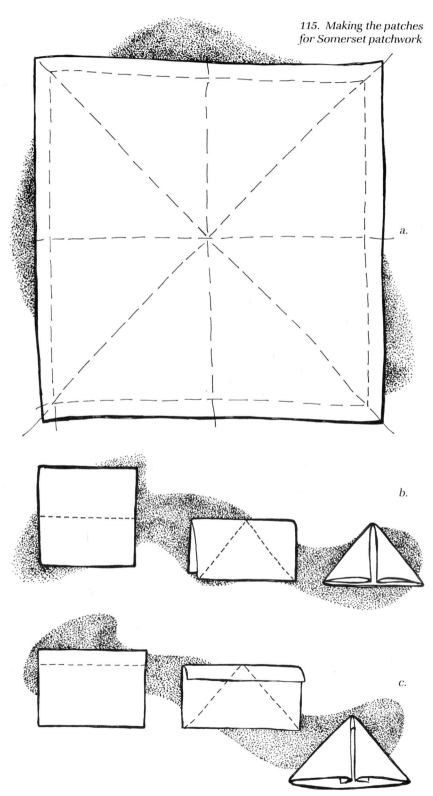

115. Making the patches for Somerset patchwork

a.

b.

c.

(above) Somerset Patchwork by Pauline Rumbold & Brenda Power

then be cut to shape and the edges bound with bias binding. If a square motif is required, add triangles as though continuing with imaginary circles until the corners are filled.

Somerset patchwork is sometimes used for quilt blocks and cushions, but is more likely to be found decorating box tops, pockets or bags.

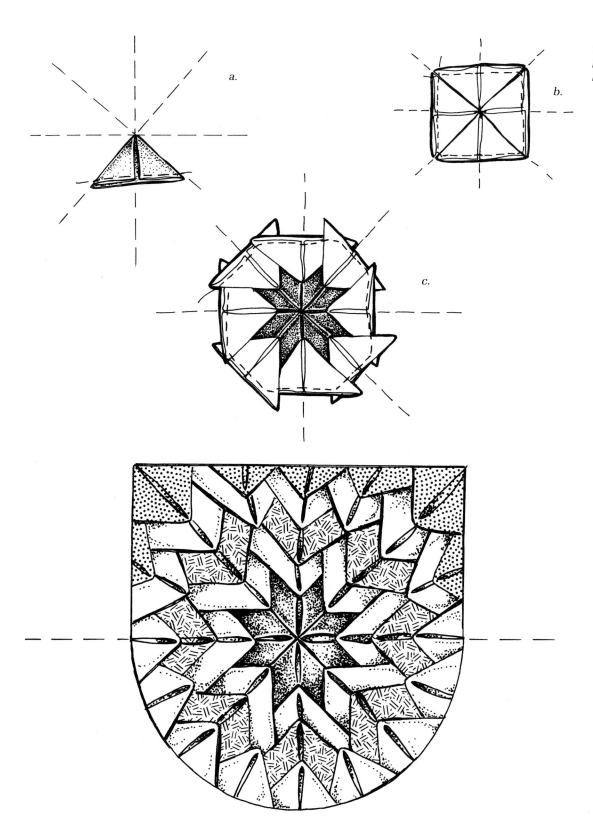

116. Assembling the patches for Somerset patchwork

a.

b.

c.

Prairie points

A variation on Somerset patchwork sometimes used as an edging is commonly known as prairie points. Here the units employed may be the same as for folded patchwork, or folded ribbon may be substituted.

Fold the units as in figure 116 but place them, side by side, between the back and front of a cushion, or between the two layers of a facing. Alternatively, they can be overlapped. Another method is to fold a square in half diagonally, and then fold diagonally again, arranging the units so that they fit into each other.

117. Prairie patches

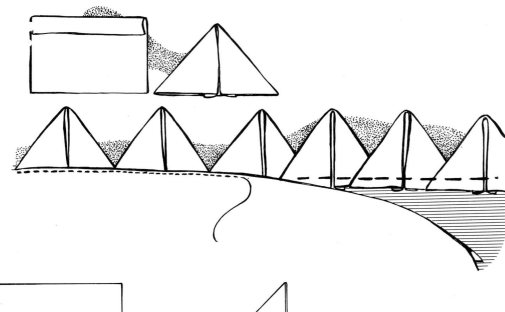

118. Prairie patches variation

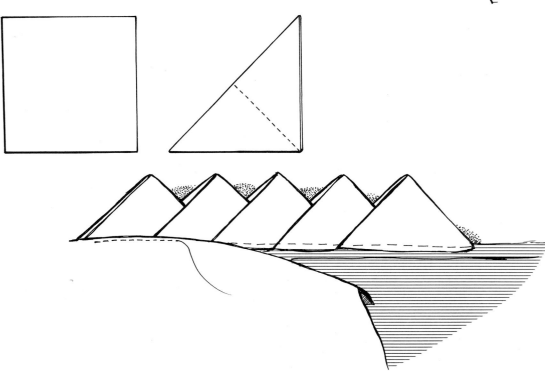

CHAPTER 8

CARE *and* CLEANING

Always try to ensure that the patchwork on which you have lavished so much care is never exposed to strong sunlight, as even the most light-fast cottons will fade in time, and the fibres will deteriorate. Never store it in plastic bags, as these can encourage mould.

If in doubt, take patchwork to a specialist cleaner where it will receive individual care. If you are sure that all the fabrics and the filling are washable, wash by hand in the bath using warm water and a mild detergent. Do not rub, and do not twist or wring to get rid of the water. Rinse well, and then squeeze out the excess water. If the spin drier will accommodate it, give it a short spin and then dry flat outdoors with a sheet underneath it, but protected from the direct sunlight.

No one book can tell you everything about patchwork, but I hope this has given you a basis on which to go forward. There are specialist books on most of the varieties of patchwork touched on here, and numerous magazines catering for the quilt addict. I have listed those which I have found most useful in the Further Reading section.

*'Signs of the Zodiac'
quilt by Wendy Bates*

*(left) 'Stellifes' by
Gisela Thwaites*

SUPPLIERS

GREAT BRITAIN

Those mainly mail order marked *

*Ashlawn Fabrics,
The Patchwork Place,
6 The Square,
Dunchurch,
Rugby, Warwickshire CV22 6NX

*The Bramble Patch,
Home Farm Barn,
Upper Stowe, Northampton. NN7 4SH

Green Hill
27, Bell Street,
Romsey, Hampshire.

The Patchwork Dog and Calico Cat,
21 Chalk Farm Road,
London, NW1.

*Quilt Basics,
31, Batchelors Way,
Amersham, Bucks. HP7 9AJ

The Quiltery,
Newey Mill,
Tipton, DY4 8AH

*Tritex Fabrics,
5–7, Fort Street,
Accrington, BB5 1OG

*Village Fabrics,
Dept. P.Q.,
30, Goldsmiths Lane,
Wallingford, Oxon. OX10 0DN

CANADA

Quilters Helper,
Box 519,
5511 Main Street,
Osgoode, Ontario. KOA 2WO

The Stitchery,
Box 338,
Olds, Alberta. TOM IP0

U.S.A.

Up to date names and addresses of suppliers
are best obtained from Quilt Magazines.

FURTHER READING

These are books I have found useful:

Elsie Svennas, *Advanced Quilting*, Scribners (Ideas)

Herta Puls, *The Art of Cutwork and Appliqué*, Batsford (Kuna Indian Patchwork)

The Complete Book of Patchwork and Quilting, W.I. Publications (general information)

Dixie Haywood, *The Contemporary Crazy Quilt Patchwork Book*, Crown Publishers (crazy patchwork)

Edna Wark, *The Craft of Patchwork*, Batsford

Dorothy Osler, *Machine Patchwork*, Batsford

Margaret Wright, *Mitred Patchwork*, Batsford (Somerset patchwork)

Maggie Malone, *1001 Patchwork Designs*, Sterling Publishing (traditional American designs)

Averil Colby, *Patchwork*, Batsford

Averil Colby, *Patchwork Quilts*, Batsford

Beth Gutcheon, *The Perfect Patchwork Primer*, Penguin (general information)

Virginia Avery, *Quilts to Wear*, Bell & Hyman (patchwork on clothing)

Janet Rae, *The Quilts of the British Isles*, Constable (historical background)

Margaret Brandebourg, *Seminole Patchwork*, Batsford

Dorothy Osler, *Traditional British Quilts*, Batsford (historical information)

Mavis Fitzrandolph, *Traditional Quilting*, Batsford

Also the following magazines:

Patchwork and Quilting (quarterly)
1 Highfield Close, Malvern Link, Worcs. WR14 1SH

Canada Quilts (5 issues a year)
P.O. Box 326, Grimsby, Ontario L3M 4G5, Canada

Quilter's Newsletter Magazine (monthly)
Box 394, Wheatridge, Colorado 80033, USA

Once you are involved with patchwork you will be amazed how many other people have been bitten by the same bug. You will find branches of the Quilters' Guild and other patchwork groups near you if you look, and they are sure to have exhibitions at least once a year.

You will find, as I have, that Quilters are a friendly lot.

GLOSSARY

Album quilt – a quilt made up of blocks of different patterns (see *sampler quilt*)

All-over quilts – quilts made with a design in geometrical shapes which are joined in a continuous pattern all over the quilt. The best known is the Hexagon, but Baby's Blocks is another example

Alphabet quilt – quilt decorated with letters of the alphabet in pieced work or appliqué, or a combination of the two

Amish quilts – quilts made by the Amish people, a religious sect who emigrated to the United States in the eighteenth and nineteenth centuries and are noted for their frugal and simple life style. Their quilts are simple in design and restrained in colour

Appliqué – the application of one piece of fabric to another, usually to make a pattern

Back or backing – the bottom layer of the quilt

Baste – see *tack*

Batting – also called wadding or fill. The fluffy material used between the top and back of a quilt to give warmth, and, by giving 'loft' to the quilting, adding to the attractiveness of the appearance of the quilt

Bedspread – decorative covering for a bed, not necessarily patched or quilted

Binding – a strip of bias cut or straight grain fabric used to enclose raw edges. The process of attaching binding

Block – the unit of design, repeated to make up a pattern on a quilt top. These are usually square, but may have other shapes

Border – the band of fabric which is sewn around the edges of a quilt to frame the basic pattern. This may be plain fabric, decorated with quilting, or a patchworked pattern

Bride quilt – in nineteenth-century America a girl would be expected to start working on quilts for her trousseau as soon as she was competent with a needle. Ideally, by the time she was of marriageable age she would have made twelve quilts. The thirteenth, adorned with hearts, flowers and bows, would be made with the assistance of her friends, only after she had become engaged to be married

Charm quilt – a one-patch quilt made up with all the patches being of different patterns of fabric, usually achieved by 'swapping' or trading with other quilters

Crazy quilt – a quilt without any repeat pattern, made up of random colours and sizes of fabric. These quilts could be made up of blocks or strips of random pieces, and are frequently embroidered but rarely quilted

Durham quilts – patchwork or wholecloth quilts made in County Durham from the seventeenth century onwards, probably the forerunners of American patchwork patterns, but noted specially for the quality of the quilting. Probably better called 'North Country Quilts', as they are not confined to County Durham

Fill – see *batting* and *wadding*

Foundation block – a plain block or piece of fabric to which pieces are sewn to form a design. Used in crazy quilts, log cabin patterns, and appliqué, for instance

Friendship quilt – a quilt made as a gift, with each block made and signed by a different person

Interlining – sometimes used instead of batting as the centre layer of a quilt. In the past a worn blanket was often used to give the extra warmth desired, and to provide the 'loft' for quilting

Lattice strips – strips of fabric used between patterned blocks to separate them

Mariner's compass – a block or quilt pattern based on an intricate star design radiating from a centre, somewhat similar to the pattern painted on eighteenth-century compasses, or the compass bearing on an elaborate map of the period

Masterpiece quilt – a particularly intricate quilt made with great skill – a status symbol more than a utilitarian object. Generally treasured in the family and used only on the most special of occasions

Medallion quilt – a quilt with a dominant central area, usually pieced, surrounded by one or more decorative borders

Mitre – a diagonal seam joining two pieces of fabric to form a corner

One-patch quilt – a quilt made using one shape only of patch. This can be a square, as in 'Irish Chain', a hexagon, as in the traditional 'Grandmother's Flower Garden', or a diamond, as in 'Tumbling' or 'Baby's Blocks'

Patch – originally a small piece of fabric sewn over a hole in a garment to repair it, this can also mean a small piece of fabric sewn onto another to form a decoration. It can mean too, in quilting parlance, a single piece of fabric which is joined to others to make up a whole pattern

Patchwork – a material which has been constructed of small pieces of fabric or other material to make up a decorative whole

Piecing – the method of joining patches together to make a pattern

Quilt – a bed-covering which has been constructed of three layers of material (usually a top and a backing with batting forming the centre layer) which are stitched together to form a whole. As a verb, it means the method of joining the three layers together

Quilt-as-you-go – the quilting of each block, individually, to be joined to others later, usually with a flat felled seam, or with binding

Quilt top – the top layer of a quilt, usually decorative

Reverse appliqué – a fabric decoration where the patch is placed behind the top fabric, the edges of the hole which it shows through being hemmed down on to it

Sampler quilt – a quilt made up of a variety of widely differing blocks, either made by the patchworker to utilize experiments, or by a teacher as a visual aid demonstrating various types of patchwork

Sashes or sashing – another name for lattice bands

Scrap quilt – a quilt made from bits of fabric accumulated from dressmaking, etc. Varieties of colours and patterns are used together instead of the more co-ordinated few purchased specially for the purpose

Set or setting – the method of sewing blocks together, i.e. a quilt 'set solid' would have patterned blocks butting

String patchwork – patterns made by joining narrow strips of left-over material to make a new patterned fabric

String sewing – machine piecing of repeats of quilt block sections, one after another, without cutting the threads, until all are sewn in pairs. They are then divided, pressed open, and assembled again for sewing to the next section of the blocks

Strip patchwork – strips sewn together to form one deep band which can then be cut into slices or pieces and resewn to make a new pattern

Tack – to sew layers or pieces together with temporary stitches, usually long running stitches

Template – a pattern used for marking the parts of a design on fabric or paper. Commercial templates can be obtained made from metal or plastic, or they may be made from stiff card, sandpaper, or special plastic sheet sold for the purpose

Throw – a small quilt, generally used as a covering for a nap, rather than as a proper quilt

Tied quilt – instead of being quilted, this is tied together at intervals. Used chiefly for very thick quilts, it is also useful where there is no time to quilt the three layers together. Where polyester batting is used it is quite successful, but woollen and cotton batts tend to 'bunch' when this method is used

Vilene – trade name for non-woven backing material. (Pellon in USA)

Wadding – see *batting*

Whole cloth quilts – quilts with the top made of one fabric with no pieced or patched decoration, usually decorated with intricate quilting

'Delectable Mountains' by Gisela Thwaites

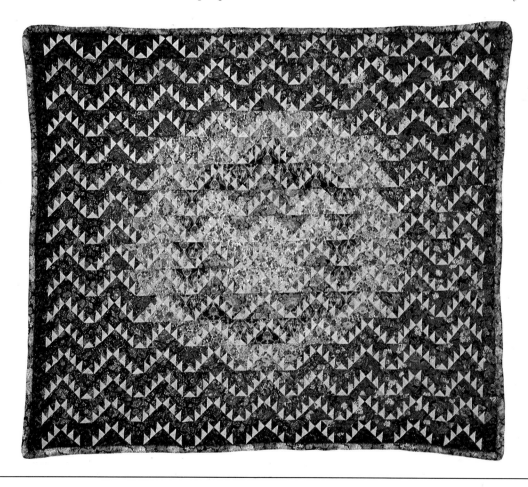

INDEX